STARTUP MINDSET: HELP ME START A BUSINESS

10 LESSONS ON HOW TO OVERCOME FEAR, LEARN THE MILLIONAIRE START-UP MINDSET, & BECOME A CONFIDENT LEADER

PETE MOON

CONTENTS

INTRODUCTION

The greatest obstacle you will face on your journey of starting and running a business won't be the lack of funding. In fact, as stressful as raising capital can be, it won't necessarily delay you in getting started.

The real obstacle you must overcome when starting and running a business is the obstacle you pose to yourself.

You know yourself better than anyone else. You are familiar with the quality of your thoughts, the purpose behind your actions, as well as the aspirations you have set for your life. You are aware of your strengths and weaknesses—even though, at times, you might hide them from the public eye.

This should be a good thing, right? After all, we are told over and over again the importance of self-awareness. While it is a good thing to be aware of who you are and how you think, it can also be the reason why starting a business terrifies you!

I can almost hear you whispering to yourself:

"I'm not qualified to be an entrepreneur."

"My life will change for the worse once I quit my nine-to-five job."

"My business idea won't survive in this competitive market."

"I'm not as cutthroat as the entrepreneurs I've seen."

Even though these self-limiting beliefs are assumptions, your mind treats them as truth because they represent what you believe. In other words, who you believe you are and what you believe you can or cannot achieve becomes what shapes your reality and sets the tone for the rest of your life.

I remember the back and forth conversations I used to have with myself about whether to pursue a career change or not. I had a stable nine-to-five job that offered me a comfortable life... except it wasn't fulfilling. The choice to leave my comfort zone and start a business wasn't an easy one. I had always been the employee, not the employer, so stepping into a leadership role felt different.

For the most part, I had to teach myself how to think and act like a leader. This meant accepting many defeats, making a ton of mistakes, and learning the lessons from each setback. It wasn't easy building a million-dollar business, but through adopting the start-up mindset, I was able to take a one-figure business and turn it into a seven-figure business over a few years.

If you have picked up this book, you have a desire to establish a start-up business. Perhaps you have always dreamed of being an entrepreneur, but due to life circumstances, the pressures of your day job, and your hesitancy to take action, your desire has remained, well, just that: a desire.

You have read the stories of successful leaders and wondered where they got the courage to take a leap of faith and build their million-dollar businesses from the ground. The truth is that it takes more than courage to start and run a business. What those successful leaders had, and what you are about to learn from this book, is how to master the start-up mindset.

No one is born with a start-up mindset. Instead, it is a mentality every entrepreneur must learn through embracing the challenges that come with starting and running a business. It takes resilience, commitment to your goals, and a positive attitude toward hard work for you to make it through the obstacles of starting a business.

The start-up mindset echoes the concept of "mind over matter." This means that your success in entrepreneurship is less about the unfavorable challenges you will face along your journey and more about your perspective on what is happening around you. By changing your mind, you can change your outlook on entrepreneurship and feel less afraid to start building your business empire today!

In this book, you will be taught the 10 lessons that every aspiring entrepreneur needs to learn when starting a new business. These lessons aren't about the technicalities of starting a business but more so about teaching you how to think like a successful business owner.

Do you believe you have what it takes to master the start-up mindset?

Well, if you believe you do, then prepare yourself for a mental shift that will change your outlook on entrepreneurship and empower you to be the kind of leader you have always dreamed of becoming!

LESSON 1: NETWORK AND PUSH DOORS

Networking is not about just connecting people. It's about connecting people with people, people with ideas, and people with opportunities.
—Michele Jennae

THE POWER OF GREAT MINDS COMING TOGETHER

A university campus is not exactly the place you would think billion-dollar ideas are created. But, when you place a group of gifted Harvard students in one room, innovations like Meta (formerly known as Facebook) are born.

Mark Zuckerberg showed a passion for computer programming from a very young age. When he was only 12 years old, he developed an interoffice communication system called Zucknet for his father to use in his dental practice. His parents enrolled him at Phillips Exeter Academy (a private prep school for gifted children), and graduating from there, he applied and got accepted into Harvard University.

Zuckerberg didn't waste any time building a name for himself in Harvard. After a short while, he was known as the go-to computer programmer students would call on if they had any computer issues. By the second year of university, he had developed two computer programs, FaceMash and CourseMatch, which became popular among students.

His reputation on campus caused other tech-minded students to be drawn to him. On one particular occasion, he was approached by some friends to partner in developing a social networking site where Harvard students could connect with each other. The site was called Facebook, and for the first few months, Zuckerberg ran it from his dorm room.

The concept exploded, and within a year, Facebook caught the attention of venture capitalists who were willing to invest millions into making the platform a global social networking site. Over the years, Facebook's market share has grown exponentially. From boasting a few hundred users in 2004 to having 2.8 billion users worldwide in 2021, the story of Facebook is a true testament to how networking can lead to the spread of ideas and business opportunities (Tarver, 2021).

FINDING THE RIGHT PEOPLE

How many people does it take to make a successful business transaction? The answer is at least two. One person is the seller, and the other is the buyer. There cannot be a successful exchange of goods or services without at least two people coming together. When you think about succeeding in business, your business network can either open doors for you or keep them shut.

Knowing a lot of businesspeople won't necessarily expose you to million-dollar ideas and opportunities. This is because not everyone in your network can be considered a valuable connection. In his book, *7 Habits of Highly Effective People,* Stephen Covey lists creating synergy as the sixth habit of highly effective people (Covey, n.d.) According to him, you can be inspired to come up with innovative ideas when you surround yourself with people who are just as passionate about ideas as you are! In essence, you feed off of the positive and ambitious energy of those around you, which causes you to expand your mind and think creatively.

Synergy is defined as the combined power of a group of individuals when they work together toward a common goal. Effective networking is all about finding people who you can collaborate with on ideas, share knowledge, and transfer skills. This means that the nature of your business relationship should be reciprocal, where both you and the other person feel like you are getting something out of the exchange. To synergize with someone else, both of you must share the following qualities:

- Common goals
- Strong sense of self (knowing who you are)
- Openness, particularly to new ideas
- Willingness to collaborate
- Willingness to take risks
- Effective communication and negotiation skills

When seeking to attract the right people, you need to be honest and ask yourself: *Am I someone that others would like to know?* The Law of Attraction states that "like attracts like," which means that things or people that are similar to one another are naturally drawn to each other. For example, if you want to attract problem-solvers, you must place yourself in environments where there are problems to solve. Or, if you want to build relationships with a certain group of people, like tech-savvy entrepreneurs, you will need to develop an interest in technology, attend tech conferences, and immerse yourself in the tech culture.

If I hadn't read a random blog, I might never have come across the business idea that became a multimillion-dollar business. I realized that if I wanted to be the next Mark Zuckerberg, I needed to expose myself to new content online so that I could explore new business ideas. Was it easy exposing myself to new information? Honestly speaking, most times, I didn't know what exactly I was looking for when browsing the internet; however, I had faith that I would intuitively know when I came across a brilliant idea. The same applied when I went out to business seminars and talks. I didn't really know who I would potentially meet in those environments, but I trusted that being around other entrepreneurial minds meant that I would walk away with some sort of value, which would allow me to become a person of value.

HOW TO IDENTIFY OPPORTUNITIES

Surrounding yourself with the right people, in the right environments, is the ideal way to find new opportunities. However, since you are only starting out in the business world, it may be difficult for you to meet the right people or be invited to certain events or boardroom meetings.

Instead of relying on certain people to open doors for you, you will need to push doors open for yourself. To do this, you need to consider the resources available to you and find ways of using what you have at your disposal to get you ahead and help you find opportunities. Reflecting back on my journey, the internet was a valuable resource I had access to that allowed me to access knowledge. There was no limit to the number of sites I could visit or the online courses I could take that could broaden my thinking. Even though reading online articles cannot replace having a lunch meeting with an expert or mentor, it was enough to help me refine my business idea.

Another free tool that many individuals have at their disposal is social media. Over the past decade, social media has become a hot spot for business networking, especially among start-up businesses seeking to build awareness of their products or services. Not only can social media platforms give you insights on your ideal customers, but they can also help you build a strong brand and manage your reputation online. There are also social media groups or clubs for business owners operating in specific industries that offer guidance, free resources, and support through the journey of growing a business. You can use social media groups for connecting with other like-minded entrepreneurs; marketing your products or services; or getting advice from experts.

As a start-up entrepreneur with a relatively small network, you will need to train your mind to look for opportunities in everyday life situations. For example, on the way to the store to buy milk, you could drive past a billboard with a catchy slogan that triggers your imagination or be inspired after having a meaningful conversation with the cashier. In other words, any experience can potentially lead to an opportunity when you are consciously looking for opportunities.

Training yourself to have an eye for opportunities requires a lot of practice. Here are some of the exercises you can practice on a regular basis to help you identify opportunities in everyday occurrences:

- If you work a nine-to-five job, start paying attention to the business processes used at work and think of ways you would improve upon those processes if you ran the company.
- When having casual conversations with friends, family, or colleagues, try to identify the pain points or unmet needs expressed in their communication.
- Watch the news or read a business newspaper and think about some of the major challenges facing your neighborhood, town, state, or country.
- Look at the customer reviews of some of the local businesses in your area and consider what these

businesses can do to improve the customers' experiences.
- Research some of the innovative products or services developed in a foreign country and think of ways you could adapt them to fit the local market.
- Consider the ways you could improve the business model of a certain industry, like transportation or tourism, by adding certain technologies.

Networking Your Way to the CEO

As a leader, there will come a point where you will need to network with other business leaders to establish partnerships or build long-term relationships. When you are acquainted with other CEOs, you are able to stay up to date with industry trends, gain access to new opportunities, and have people you can turn to for business support.

But here's the dilemma that many start-up entrepreneurs face: How do you network with business leaders who are just as busy as you are?

Indeed, networking with any high-level executive isn't easy because, as you may know, the higher your position, the less accessible you become. You might be fortunate to attend the same networking event as another business leader, but try scheduling an hour meeting with them, and you'll be told they are unavailable.

So what can you do? The best way to network with other business leaders is to reach out to a few connectors rather than directly going to the source. Connectors are people who have a large network of business contacts and are able to help you make introductions and get in front of the businesspeople you desire to connect with. Note that connectors may be people you already know, such as an uncle or cousin who has experience in a particular industry, used to work at a particular company, or is part of a particular social club or group.

If you are familiar with the business networking site, LinkedIn, you will understand how valuable connectors can be in expanding your network and connecting with the right people. Your network on LinkedIn consists of first-, second-, and third-degree connectors. Your first-degree connectors are people, mostly colleagues and friends, who you know on a personal level. Your second-degree connectors are people who are connected to your first-degree connector. In other words, both you and your second-degree connector have a mutual acquaintance. Your third-degree connectors are people who are connected to your second-degree connector. Here, there is no mutual connection established; however, your third-degree connector still falls in as part of your larger network.

You can apply the same concept when networking your way to the CEO. Consider the company or industry the targeted CEO works at. Next, think of the first-degree connectors you know within that company or industry who can get you in the door. If you are fortunate enough, you might have a friend or former work colleague who has indirect access to the CEO you seek to connect with.

Set up a meeting with your first-degree connector and ask them to introduce you to your second-degree connector (the individual who they are connected with who can get you one step closer to the CEO). The second-degree connector might not have direct access to the CEO, but they at least know someone who does—in other words, they know your third-degree connector who may be in an even better position to introduce you to the CEO. The networking chain would continue until you eventually connect with someone, like the personal assistant or company director, who can help you schedule a meeting with the CEO.

Now that you have a strategy for reaching the top man or woman in any organization, you will need a few tips to help you approach them with confidence and make your request. Here are five tips to remember when connecting with CEOs:

1. Be Clear About What You Want

It's worth mentioning again that any individual in an executive position doesn't have a lot of time to spare. Therefore, you need to be clear and direct about the purpose for reaching out to them. Before scheduling the meeting, think about your desired outcome for your new business relationship. Do you want to partner with them on a business idea? Do you need a referral or mentorship? Write down all of the reasons you are interested in connecting with them and make you present them early on in your discussion or in a formal email.

2. Build Your Professional Reputation

When growing your network, many people will be interested to know who you are and what you are about. Instead of coming directly to you, the first place people will search for your name is on the internet. Having a professional LinkedIn profile can make it easier for people to find you and learn more about your business. You can also gain more credibility by having a business website or blog that can be found through a quick Google search. Even though you can't control what others think of you, you can at least manage your personal brand as a leader so that what others see or read about you represents your values, goals, and mission.

3. Study Other Leaders

If you want to know how successful leaders handle themselves online and offline, why not read an autobiography, watch some of their interviews, or follow them on social media? They say that imitation is the best kind of compliment you can pay someone, and I certainly have to agree. You can learn a lot of valuable tricks on how to communicate with other leaders by observing how successful leaders communicate and carry themselves in conversations. If you follow them on social media, you can also learn tips on how to build your personal brand as a leader and the type of content to post. By following in the footsteps of the greatest orators, negotiators, and leaders of our time, you can develop the necessary skills to walk into any room and speak confidently to anyone.

4. Avoid Acting Like an Underdog

As a leader, you want to be respected by your peers in your chosen field. To earn the respect of other business leaders, you need to present yourself as an equal. This means avoiding acting like an underdog. Yes, of course, you are new to the business world, and there is still much for you to learn. However, that doesn't mean you don't deserve a seat at the boardroom table or to be around entrepreneurs who are more successful and experienced than you. When you come across other leaders who are not willing or interested to help you with your requests, simply move on and approach other leaders. You never have to beg anyone for an opportunity or compromise your values or principles to be accepted into certain circles. Surround yourself with people who respect you and acknowledge the value you bring to the table.

5. Remember That It's Just Business

There is nothing more disappointing than being rejected by an individual you had hopes of working with or getting to know on a personal level. However, to survive on your journey of networking, it's important not to take rejection personally. Remember that at the end of the day, business is a game, and the leaders who play well end up winning. If you come across a CEO who isn't interested in getting to know you, chances are they don't believe you have anything to offer them. Instead of trying to win them over, you can work on developing yourself as a leader and growing your business so that the same person who rejected you requests an hour of your time. In the business world, decisions aren't made based on emotions but rather on logic. If the networking opportunity isn't a win-win for both parties, there is a low chance that a business relationship will be formed.

IT'S ALWAYS A NO IF YOU DON'T ASK—HOW TO ASK FOR MENTORSHIP FROM A SUCCESSFUL BUSINESS LEADER

Other than seeking assistance with your business, you may also reach a point where you seek support and guidance from a seasoned entrepreneur. Let's face it: Maintaining a start-up business for more than a year isn't easy, especially if this is your first rodeo. There will be times when you cup your face in your hands in disbelief of your current situation or how you will possibly get yourself out of it.

During the low points of starting and running your start-up, you will need a special type of confidante, like a mentor, who can offer you sound business advice and keep you focused on your goals. As valuable as it is having a mentor, they are difficult to find. This is because mentors are usually experienced experts or entrepreneurs who live busy lives. Even after identifying someone who would make for a great mentor, they might not have the luxury of time to meet with you on a regular basis or play an active role on your entrepreneurial journey.

Asking someone to be your mentor is also not an easy task. For the most part, if you genuinely desire for someone to coach you on your journey, the last thing you will want to hear from them is a big "No." You might be able to take rejection from your peers or disapproving customers, but when it comes from someone you admire, it can be painful. However, the only thing worse than being told no by a potential mentor is not making your request known in the first place.

I grew up being told that if you don't ask, the answer is always no. The fear of not approaching an individual due to the possibility of being rejected is the only thing standing in your way of making a valuable connection. Prepare yourself in advance for whatever the expert might say. If their answer is no, cross their name off your list and prepare yourself to contact the next individual. The truth is that not every person you desire to be a part of your network will either want to or have the time to build a business relationship with you. This is all part of the game of networking, and only those who play end up winning!

Now that the possibility of getting rejected by a mentor feels less overwhelming, here are some of the steps you can take when approaching individuals seeking mentorship:

1. Decide Whether You Need Mentorship

Not every entrepreneur will benefit from having a mentor. Why do I say this? It's because each entrepreneur has a unique vision for how they desire to enrich themselves and develop as a leader. For some entrepreneurs, mentorship could be an opportunity to learn from the leaders in the industry and follow after their footsteps, while other entrepreneurs might prefer learning through lived experiences and the personal failures and victories they have encountered.

There are also other ways to acquire knowledge other than being coached by another person. For instance, you could read personal development and business books; enroll in business-related online courses; or get some on-the-job training. The point here is that you should only consider mentorship if it is something that you feel would benefit you as an entrepreneur and make your journey less overwhelming.

2. Identify Potential Mentors

If mentorship is something you are interested in, the next step would be to identify potential mentors. Not everybody who has years of experience as an entrepreneur is necessarily "mentor material." In other words, just because someone is knowledgeable about a certain aspect of life doesn't mean they would make good teachers or role models. When identifying potential mentors, start by thinking about businesspeople within your network that have shown some kind of interest in your journey as a leader in the past.

Through the conversations you have shared, they might have given you an indication that you can call them, schedule lunch, or ask business-related questions whenever you like. Approaching people who have already shown interest in you can reduce the likelihood of rejection dramatically. In fact, you may even be surprised that these people have been secretly hoping to one day share a few business lessons with you!

After identifying these people, you would then need to go through a process of elimination by assessing how many of the other criteria they meet. For example, how much experience in the business world does each person have? What skills or qualifications do they have? Where have they worked and in which positions? How well do you "click" with each of them? Ideally, if you find at least one person who meets all of your criteria, consider yourself fortunate. However, don't feel disappointed if the people you have access to only meet a few criteria.

3. Make Your Request Clear

This step won't be difficult if you approach an individual who is already a part of your network, and you have already laid the foundation in building your relationship. At most, it will feel like asking one of your peers for a favor—less intimidating than asking for help from a stranger. Nevertheless, you will still need to be direct when asking them to be your mentor. You can start the conversation by mentioning the value you have seen in them and how they have influenced your entrepreneurial journey in the short amount of time you have known them.

Next, explain the kind of relationship you would like to have with them and what it would entail. For example, you might ask to see them once a month for a coffee; express your openness to receive advice or feedback; or ask them to hold you accountable to your goals. You can even go as specific as detailing how many minutes or hours of their time you will need per month, where your meeting place will be, what you expect out of each meeting, and so forth. Remember that the other individual may or may not be able to provide you with everything you hope for in a mentor-mentee relationship, and once again, this is perfectly normal. If you are able to reach a compromise, then it's better than walking away without any assistance at all.

4. Nurture Your Mentoring Relationship

When you have secured a mentor, your mentor-mentee relationship has only just begun. It is up to you from this point onward to nurture this relationship, ensuring that you fulfill all of the obligations you had agreed on and make your mentor's job a lot easier. You want your mentor to look forward to meeting with you and being a part of your journey—no matter how big or small their role may be. You also want them to feel like they are adding value to your career and aren't wasting any of their precious time. Nurturing the mentoring relationship can open you up to referrals, business opportunities, and wisdom you couldn't learn in any business school.

The best way to show your mentor that you respect their time is being prepared for each meeting. Create an agenda of all the topics you would like to speak about during your session with your mentor. If you have any questions you would like to ask, have them written down on a piece of paper beforehand. During the first few meetings with your mentor, you may struggle to find topics to speak about or questions to ask. Don't fret: Below are some of the general questions that will help you build rapport with your mentor and kick-start your mentoring relationship:

- How did you develop the discipline to get to the level where you are?
- What is the one piece of advice you would give a start-up entrepreneur in my position?
- What kind of skills should I be developing to accelerate my career?
- What are some of the major distractions that set you back when you were building your career/business?
- How can I achieve a good work-life balance?
- What are some of the coping strategies you use to reduce stress?
- What are some of the sacrifices you had to make early on to achieve your goals?
- Do you have any tips for expanding my network?
- What do you expect from me as a mentee?
- What strengths and weaknesses have you already identified in me?
- Are there any books you would like me to read?

- Do you have any feedback on how I can improve my communication skills?
- Do you have any tips on how I can remain competitive in my industry?
- What are some of the daily habits I can adopt to develop my leadership skills?

LESSON 2: SAY YES TO TAKING RISKS

When you walk to the edge of all the light you have and take that first step into the darkness of the unknown, you must believe that one of two things will happen. There will be something solid for you to stand upon or you will be taught to fly.

—Patrick Overton

LIFE IS A RISK

Being an entrepreneur is a risky endeavor. You are probably aware of this if you have ever tried to start a business in the past and seen just how much work being a leader entails. However, deciding to become an entrepreneur isn't the riskiest decision you will make in your life. In fact, if we were to assess the risk level associated with entrepreneurship, it would probably be a 6 out of 10. Other personal life commitments you will make—like deciding to start a family, having children, or relocating to a new country—carry far greater risks than starting and running a business.

If this doesn't put your mind at ease, perhaps you might appreciate this fact: Everything that lies beyond your comfort zone is technically risky because you don't have the experience to face it.

You have lived a comfortable life for many years and committed yourself to a safe and predictable routine:

- Wake up
- Eat breakfast
- Travel to work
- Travel back home
- Eat dinner with your family
- Go to sleep

Your routine is familiar, and at no point has it offered you the kinds of challenges necessary for growth. That is why you are reading this book. There is a deep part of you that recognizes the need for a challenge, but since you have never placed yourself in a position to be challenged, you are afraid of it. In essence, you are both deathly afraid and excited about the idea of stepping out of your comfort zone and working toward your dream of becoming an entrepreneur.

Don't worry: You don't sound crazy to me. A few years ago, I was in your position. Nothing made me cringe more than waking up and commuting to work. There was nothing I enjoyed about my day job, and during my breaks, I would often fantasize about handing in my resignation and starting my own business. However, I was equally terrified of leaving the security of a stable income. But challenging myself meant more than losing myself in a predictable but unfulfilling life. For the first time, I was ready to accept the risk of a career change and everything else that came with it!

From the moment you stepped into the world, you proved how much of a risk life really is. On the night you were conceived, 40 million sperm swam toward an egg, but only one survived. To say that you are one in a million would be an accurate statement. You spent the following nine months in your mother's womb developing into a human being. Your survival in the womb wasn't any less risky than your survival outside of the womb. As an infant, you intuitively understood the risk of not being able to integrate yourself into this world. To mitigate the risk, you began teaching yourself how to behave like a human by watching your parents and modeling everything they did. Soon, you were able to walk, speak, laugh, and enjoy other human experiences.

Being an adult hasn't made life any less risky. From my own experience, I had to learn the hard way that whether I committed myself to my goals or not, I would still be faced with challenges I was never prepared for. I figured that if risk was always going to be a factor in my life—comfort zone or not—it would be better for me to live a life with no regrets in spite of the risks I would be exposed to.

What a liberating revelation this was for me. Even though it didn't make my decision to leave my day job any easier, it at least removed the fear that was standing in my way of choosing to become an entrepreneur. Several years later, being an entrepreneur is still a risk I choose to take every single day, and so far, I am proud of the decision I made.

COMMON RISKS OF STARTING A BUSINESS

Success in the business world comes as a result of taking calculated risks. When a business launches a new product, for example, the product could be a hit or miss. The product may not be appropriate for the market; customers may not be impressed by its price or design; or the technology may be outdated. Or by the stroke of genius and luck, the product could become the hottest trend on the market, and it could single-handedly turn you into a millionaire.

What makes entrepreneurship risky are the two extremities: It can either become your gateway to wealth or drive you into debt. Nevertheless, the risk is still worth taking for those who have a solid plan of action, the correct mindset, and an unshakeable passion for business.

When cultivating a start-up mindset, it's important to be honest with yourself about what you are getting into. Glossing over the potential risks you might face as a start-up entrepreneur is a recipe for disaster. To reduce as much risk as possible, you need to acknowledge the nature of business and gain knowledge on the types of risks you could be exposed to, so you can make the necessary preparations to mitigate risk in advance. Below are some of the common risks of starting a business:

1. Financial Risk

Start-up businesses need funding. If you are fortunate enough to have a lump sum of cash in savings, you may not feel the pinch of investing capital into your business. However, the average entrepreneur doesn't have a lot of money to invest up front, which could mean having to borrow money from friends or financial institutions to get the business off the ground. The risk in funding a start-up business is that you are not guaranteed to receive a return on your investment. For various reasons, your business may not be able to generate revenue as fast as you would like—if any at all. The worst-case scenario would be going bankrupt after long periods of not generating enough income to pay off your debt.

Risk management plan: The best way to avoid cash flow problems or going into bankruptcy would be to create a realistic financial plan during the early stages of your business, with projections of the income and expenses for each month, until you break even. If it will take you many years before you break even, then the risk associated with starting and running that business venture may be too high.

2. Strategic Risk

Every business has a plan of action, but not every plan can bring about business success. Industries are constantly evolving, technology is becoming more sophisticated, and customer needs influence the demands of the markets. This means that although your business strategy may look good on paper, it may not be as dynamic and effective in practice.

Risk management plan: Be open and willing to adapt your business model, systems, and operations to the current trends in the market. This will ensure you remain competitive and stand at the forefront of transformation in your industry. If you are not an expert in your field, reach out to people who are and seek guidance on how you can make your business as relevant to the times as possible.

3. Market Risk

Sometimes, cash flow isn't the cause of business failure. There are times when the product or service offered by the business is simply not a fit for the market. As innovative as an idea can be, the market decides whether or not it is valuable and worth paying for. Factors affecting market demands include the economic status, market trends, consumer purchasing behaviors, openness to technology, and education about the product or service.

Risk management plan: While researching your business idea, make sure that you carry out a market analysis. This will help you assess market factors in your neighborhood, city, or state, and determine whether consumers are in need of your particular product or service offering. Remember that, in some cases, the product or service isn't necessarily bad; the market just may not be ready for it.

4. Competitor Risk

You will always come across competition in business because in every industry, there are multiple businesses with similar offerings. And, if you don't find any competition, it could be a sign that there isn't a market demand for your products or services. Having competitors becomes risky when the market you are competing in is saturated, meaning there are few large businesses offering the same products or services with little to no room for smaller businesses to compete. Moreover, since these larger businesses have more resources readily available, they tend to have a competitive advantage.

Risk management plan: Conduct a competitor analysis and study the major business players in your industry and local area. Take time to analyze their product or service offerings and how they have positioned themselves in the market. You should be able to find their strengths and weaknesses as well as opportunities for you to fill a gap. If there isn't a gap to fill, you may need to consider choosing a different market or targeting a different customer segment.

5. Reputation Risk

The reputation of a business can be the make-or-break factor when attracting new customers. Nowadays, all it takes to decide whether to support a business is scrolling through its social media pages or reading customer reviews online. The general public makes assumptions about a business whether the business owner is aware of it or not. While it's not always possible to manage public opinion, the best a business can do is prioritize customer satisfaction and operate in ways that are consistent with its brand and values.

Risk management plan: Do your best to create a brand that appeals to your target audience. Through your brand, build real relationships with your customers and offer personalized experiences. Even though it is difficult to manage your reputation, having an authentic brand and being customer-centric can help you build a positive reputation.

WHEN RISKS BECOME WORTHY SACRIFICES

When many people consider the role of a leader, they think of the power, prestige, and wealth that comes with it. Of course, there are many perks that come with operating a business, such as a better standard of living, but this isn't all there is to being a leader. What is often overlooked is the less glamorous side of leadership, which is the sacrifices that are made to get to the top.

Making a sacrifice can be defined as the act of giving up something for the sake of something else. Most of the time, the value of the sacrifice signifies the value of what is to be gained. For example, an individual who desires to lose weight will sacrifice eating their favorite desserts to achieve a certain goal weight. Giving up their favorite foods isn't easy, but it is worth the value of the desired outcome.

Behind the scenes, entrepreneurs make a lot of sacrifices, such as sacrificing a stable job, consistent income, social status, family time, and a life's worth of savings. Making these sacrifices is a risk because there is no guarantee that they will lead to the desired outcome of business success. However, the only way for them to know if the sacrifices would be worth it is to make them and live a life with no regrets.

You have a desire to start a business. It remains purely a desire until you decide to take action. But taking action comes with its own terms and conditions, like being willing to take on risks. If you believe the risks are worth taking, then what you end up losing becomes a worthy sacrifice that you make in order to grow your business. When a risk becomes a worthy sacrifice, giving up something, even if it is your hard-earned money, doesn't feel as painful as if you were not open to taking the risk in the first place. In other words, when you are able to justify risks in your mind and heart, then it stops becoming a risk altogether—it becomes something you need to do to get ahead.

Along my entrepreneurial journey, I have lost tens of thousands of dollars. I also spent many years isolated from my friends and family due to the amount of time my business demanded of me. There were several occasions when failure meant I had to go back to the drawing board and refine my business idea, and this wasted a lot of time and money. Yet, despite how risky my business journey has been, I have no regrets. Why? To me, I counted the risks as worthy sacrifices for the successful business I have today. Had it not been for the rejection, isolation, money problems, or failure, I wouldn't have the wealth of knowledge and experience necessary to run a million-dollar business.

If you are still wondering if the risk of entrepreneurship is worth it, ask yourself if you are willing to make the sacrifices for your business to succeed. If you aren't willing to make the sacrifices, then perhaps the risks associated with entrepreneurship are too great for you. But, if you are determined to give up something now for the promise of something greater in the future, then taking risks is worth it!

QUESTIONS TO DECIPHER IF ENTREPRENEURSHIP IS FOR YOU

There is an age-old debate of whether entrepreneurs are born or made. Are there people who have innate leadership qualities and are naturally resilient, or are leadership qualities and traits like resilience developed through willpower and experience? To put this debate to rest, let's think about what it takes to become an entrepreneur. Here is a list of 10 traits that every successful entrepreneur needs:

1. Optimism
2. Confidence
3. Independence
4. Creativity
5. Curiosity
6. Resilience
7. Discipline
8. Competitivity
9. Openness
10. Generosity

People are not born with these traits; rather, they are cultivated through lived experiences and sheer dedication. Therefore, even someone who never displayed any leadership qualities at school or during their younger professional years can still cultivate the qualities needed to be a successful entrepreneur.

However, there is a caveat: While you may have the qualities to become a successful business owner, entrepreneurship may still not be for you. You may have dreams of running your own empire, monopolizing an industry, or creating an international business, but the game of entrepreneurship may not be suitable for you. This is because it takes a whole lot of perseverance to endure the highs and lows of the business world, and there will be times when it makes more sense to quit than to stay in the game. But if you are led with your heart—not your mind—your passion for what you do will help you keep going.

Before we proceed to the following chapter, here are a few

reflective questions you can ask yourself to determine if entrepreneurship is for you:

1. Why do you want to be an entrepreneur?
2. How open are you to stepping out of your comfort zone?
3. How do you handle rejection?
4. How is the condition of your mental and physical health?
5. What professional sacrifices are you willing to make to succeed?
6. What personal sacrifices are you willing to make to succeed?
7. Are you motivated by your head or your heart?
8. What would it mean to give up your dream of being an entrepreneur?
9. Are you willing to grow as an individual?
10. Are you willing to make mistakes?

LESSON 3: DON'T JUST DREAM IT —DO IT

The best way to not feel hopeless is to get up and do something. Don't wait for good things to happen to you. If you go out and make some good things happen, you will fill the world with hope, you will fill yourself with hope.
—Barack Obama

FROM RAGS TO RICHES

John Paul DeJoria was raised by his mother in a single-parent household until she could no longer take care of him and handed him over to foster care. When he was old enough to look after himself, DeJoria left foster care and started looking for jobs. His financial situation got so dire that at some point, he lived out of his car. Nevertheless, his negative circumstances didn't stop him from trying to earn a living.

When he was in between jobs, DeJoria would find small products to sell. He went from selling Christmas cards to selling encyclopedias—literally anything that would help him make money and save toward college. He kept hustling throughout his 20s until eventually, he established a hair care business called John Paul

Mitchell Systems with a meager $700. His company grew as a result of word-of-mouth advertising and securing lucrative deals with hair salons. After two years, his hair care business was valued for millions of dollars, and today, it is worth billions!

When asked in an interview about his rise to the top, DeJoria said, "If you expect free lunch to come your way, you're not going to go far and you'll be very bored. Go out there and do something. Get involved" (Pierre-Bravo, 2018).

What can we learn from DeJoria's entrepreneurial journey? While there are many lessons we can take from DeJoria, perhaps the most important is this: You can't sit on your ideas. You need to get out there and do something. If you hear many of the stories of successful entrepreneurs, you'll notice that many of them didn't have a lot of money, support, or experience starting out. All they had was an idea that they believed in and the determination to see their plans through.

The value of an idea is seen in its implementation. Without actually testing out your strategies, how would you know they are viable? It's like a boat that never leaves the harbor—it is practically useless. Boats are not built to stay in the harbor; they are built to travel across oceans. For a boat to serve its purpose, it needs to be cast off from the dock and allowed to cruise on the waters. Don't just dream of adventure—just do it! You can always alter your course later, but you won't go anywhere if you just sit on your ideas or look to others to help you.

TURNING A VISION INTO REALITY

What is one business idea you have always kept at the back of your mind but haven't implemented yet?

The fact that your business idea is still a thought means that it is far from becoming a reality. For any idea to become something real and tangible, there must be action backing it up. It might feel good to fantasize about one day owning a successful business that you can pass down to your children, but unless you have a plan on how you will make this happen, it will remain a fantasy. Turning a vision into reality isn't as complicated as some may make it seem. In fact, it can be achieved in five simple steps:

Step 1: Be Clear on What You Want

Business success looks different to everyone. Not everyone dreams of creating an empire or listing their company on the stock market. For some, having a thriving community business is the definition of success. It's important to clarify what you want out of your entrepreneurial journey. Think about what business success would look like for you and consider the various milestones you would need to achieve to get there.

Step 2: Believe In Your Vision

You are the only person who can do the work required to make a business out of an idea. No one else will have as much determination and faith in your plans as you do. This is why you must ensure you are passionate about your vision enough to justify the sacrifices you will have to make to turn it into a reality. Consider the risks and costs of actively pursuing your vision. Are these risks and costs things you are capable of living with?

Step 3: Just Do It!

Step one and two is preparation, but there is only so much preparation you can do before you start taking action. At the end of the day, people won't remember those who had good ideas but instead those whose ideas positively changed their lives. The reason we speak about Steve Jobs years after his passing is because we have all, to some degree, been positively impacted by his innovations. It was his courageous action that has made him a household name today and for many years to come. Don't wait until you *feel* ready to take action. Trust me: Fear and self-doubt will be constant emotions you feel throughout your journey. Your decision to take action should be based on your vision and objectives—not your emotions.

Step 4: Create a Priority List

There are many small and major tasks you will need to do when getting started on your business. However, not every task carries the same weight of importance. For example, creating a market analysis takes greater priority than registering your business name or printing out branded T-shirts. Therefore, you need to decide on what you will tackle first and how you will do it. The best way to organize and prioritize your tasks is to group similar tasks into clusters. You can even name each cluster to make it easier to remember them. From each cluster, select one task that is extremely important. That will be the task you focus on for the next few weeks or months. This means that if you have five clusters, there will be five top-priority tasks that you focus on for the next few weeks or months.

Step 5: Review Your Progress

Monitoring how far or close you are to manifesting your vision is just as important as setting objectives. If you don't measure your progress, you won't know whether your actions are paying off. Moreover, you shouldn't wait until you make a mistake to see how you are doing. Set aside time every week or month to review the various steps you have taken to achieve your vision. You can also set business milestones that will serve as positive reminders to show you are on the right track. It is also perfectly normal to adjust or change your plans when you feel like you are going at a slow pace or moving in the wrong direction.

YOU WILL NEVER FEEL READY

Before starting my business, I had a lot of doubts. I didn't want to start a business that would end up being closed down after a year or two or make me regret leaving my stable day job. I stalled for a few years, finding various excuses for not starting my business. If it wasn't economic conditions, I was blaming my financial situation or my family responsibilities. The excuses kept changing until eventually, I realized I would never feel ready to start my business.

Unfortunately, I would never wake up one morning and feel like it was the right time to take the leap of faith. There was just too much risk associated with starting a business for me to ever feel comfortable going along with it. If I was truly passionate about making this career move, I would have to do it unprepared! That doesn't mean I wouldn't do my research and test my business idea, but it meant that I wasn't going to feel 100% ready for what I was about to take on.

Since opportunities are found outside of the comfort zone, there will always be an element of mystery that comes with them. For instance, you might have an amazing new concept for a product, but because this product doesn't exist in the market, you will never really know for sure whether customers will love it. This doesn't mean you shouldn't grab the opportunity and see it through since it could just be a million-dollar concept. What it means is that you will need to pursue the opportunity without the certainty that it could work out.

You need to say "Yes" to possibilities and figure out the details later. You will have plenty of time to plan your course of action and revise your strategies. Embrace the challenges that come with growing your business and advancing from one level to the next. There will never come a time where you aren't feeling scared because with growth comes new experiences that you have never dealt with before. See the challenges you face as chances to reinvent yourself as a leader, empower yourself with knowledge, or expand your network. You won't regret saying "Yes," but you might regret closing the door on opportunities by saying "No."

QUESTIONS TO HELP YOU CREATE A VISION FOR YOUR BUSINESS

The simplest question to ask yourself before you start a business is: *What do I want?* However, there are other in-depth questions that can help you design your ideal vision for your business. At the end of the day, you are starting a business because it means something to you to have one. Perhaps you have grown up in a family of entrepreneurs or have become inspired by a successful leader to start your own business. Your vision for your business will reflect your influences, beliefs, and aspirations that have stirred up a passion for entrepreneurship; therefore, give yourself enough room to dream big—after all, you wouldn't agree to such a huge undertaking if you didn't expect extraordinary outcomes.

Here are a few questions you can reflect on that will help you create a meaningful vision for your business:

- What drives you to start a business?
- If money wasn't a factor, what would your ideal business be like?
- What are your secret dreams that you hope to fulfill through owning a business?
- What do you want your business culture to feel like?
- What values do you want your business to stand for?

- What personal talents do you want to leverage for your business?
- How do you want to feel about yourself as a leader?
- How do you plan on impacting your community?
- What legacy do you want to leave behind through your business?

LESSON 4: MAKE LEARNING YOUR LIFELONG GOAL

Those people who develop the ability to continuously acquire new and better forms of knowledge that they can apply to their work and to their lives will be the movers and shakers in our society for the indefinite future.
—Brian Tracy

WHAT IS CONTINUOUS LEARNING?

When you were a child, you probably got bored at how many times people, particularly adults, would ask you what you wanted to be when you got older. Nonetheless, you happily answered their question, each time thinking about new career possibilities. At one moment, you may have wanted to be a truck driver, and the next moment, you were obsessed with the idea of being a fireman.

During your teenage years, the same career question was asked, this time with a more serious tone. Your parents or teachers were interested to know which career path you would take. It was no longer considered cute to say you wanted to be a truck driver or a fireman without taking other factors like skill, income, and experience into consideration. Eventually, when you graduated from high school or college, your options had been narrowed down to one or two career paths, and this was the job or field you were expected to remain in for the rest of your life.

Like any young person, I fell into the trap of thinking that my career options were limited, and because I never studied a certain subject, I couldn't explore career options in that field. My one-career-for-a-lifetime perspective caused me to settle for a predictable career and hardly ever expand my skill sets or acquire fresh knowledge. I had become stagnant and miserable, feeling like I would eventually rot in the same office cubicle doing the same uninspiring work.

The turning point was picking up self-improvement books, which awakened my sense of curiosity. I became curious about the systems of the world, the meaning behind work, and how I wanted to spend the rest of my life. I was also introduced to the concept of continuous learning: The persistence in developing your competencies and growing through acquired learning—a commitment that you could make to integrate learning into your lifestyle and constantly develop your personal and professional life.

The day you graduated from college or university may have been the last time you opened a book. This could be because you assumed the pursuit of knowledge would be confined to educational institutions. You may have also felt that after obtaining a qualification, you knew enough to face various personal and professional challenges. However, the truth is learning doesn't start and end at school. There are so many different ways to pursue knowledge outside of a textbook or manual. For example, in your adult life, you can learn new information through:

- daily interactions with people
- reading informative newspapers and magazines
- following current affairs

- online courses
- mentorship and coaching
- social media monitoring
- listening to a podcast
- monitoring the performance of various industries
- reading different book genres
- attending seminars, exhibitions, training workshops, and conferences

As an aspiring entrepreneur, continuous learning is something that can help you improve your business and leadership style. It forces you to constantly think on your feet and not rely on traditional methods and rules to solve modern problems. When you are continuously learning new skills and absorbing new information, you can also find ways to remain competitive. You stay up to date with the latest news and trends in your particular industry, which helps you adapt to the ever-changing environment.

Productive Habits for Continuous Learning

Being a lifelong student is all about having a hunger for knowledge. It doesn't necessarily need to be knowledge based on your industry. You can seek knowledge on various subjects, fields, or phenomena. A lifeline student is also about constantly adapting your approach to solving problems and finding new ways to face obstacles. This makes you agile and flexible to change.

The survival of your business rests on how much knowledge you are willing to absorb and how quickly you can adapt to changing market or economic circumstances. For example, you may have an amazing business plan, but after a shift in the market, those strategies become outdated. What do you do? The best solution would be to learn which direction the market is headed and find a way to be one of the businesses at the forefront of this change. Below are some of the productive habits you can start practicing in your business, so you can continuously learn new things:

1. Surround Yourself With Knowledgeable People

Networking isn't only useful when you are seeking assistance. Your network can also transfer skills and knowledge. In a scientific experiment, a rat was placed in a maze on its own and given a puzzle. Two more rats were placed in another maze together and given the same puzzle. The rats that were placed in the same maze together developed neurons quicker than the rat that was solving the puzzle alone. This experiment proves the old adage: There is strength in numbers. If you are in a pursuit of knowledge, the best place to seek knowledge would be within your network. Reach out to experts or sit with a few entrepreneurs, discuss ideas, and share your experiences coming from different career fields and backgrounds.

2. Learn to Filter Through Information

David Allen created a task management system called Getting Things Done (GTD) because he believed that when you have a lot of information scattered in your mind, you can have a difficult time prioritizing what's important and what isn't (Scroggs, n.d.) Even though continuous learning is about absorbing more information, you need to be selective about what information to store in your memory. Storing the wrong information or looking in the wrong places can actually become a huge distraction and hindrance to your productivity. Allen's process of getting things done and avoiding distractions is to record all of the information that is on your mind on paper or digitally and break each one into actionable work tasks with set time limits. This is known as a "mind sweep."

A mind sweep will help you create a list of the things you need to work on immediately, things to remember in the future, or the things you can mentally discard.

3. Automate Your Learning

For learning to be a part of your lifestyle, you need to integrate it into your everyday routine. What better way to integrate learning in your routine than to put it on your mobile device or laptop? Automation uses data and computer algorithms to help you filter through information and curate your news feeds so that you only see information from preferred websites and other sources. This can save you a lot of time looking for information since your computer does all of the selecting and sorting on your behalf. Data aggregation software, like Trifacta, can help you gather information from multiple sources and combine it in one place for easier filtering, data analysis, and reporting.

4. Learn in Small Intervals

Instead of trying to cram a lot of information in a single sitting, you are more likely to process information better when your learning is spaced out. You can create time blocks each day where you spend time exploring a subject, reading a book, or catching up on current affairs. During this time, practice taking pauses, so you can reflect on what you have read or heard before moving on. If the new information triggers an idea or thought, stop for a moment and follow your train of thought. You can even take a few seconds to jot down any keywords, themes, or ideas that you would like to explore in depth later on.

5. Reflect on Your Learning

After learning something new, take time to summarize what you have learned and how it could possibly relate to your personal or professional life. For example, if you hear on the radio that the price of fuel is rising, think about how that information could affect your career, home life, health, and so on. Make it a habit to assess the significance of what you learn because many times, extraordinary business innovations lie in everyday life circumstances. You can also reflect on your learning by finding someone who you can share your knowledge with. Speaking about what you have learned is a form of repetition, which gives you another opportunity to absorb and store information in your long-term memory.

ENTREPRENEURIAL SKILLS YOU NEED TO LEARN

Besides doing your research and compiling your business plan, you should continuously work toward acquiring certain skills that will help you run a successful business. If you don't have a business degree, then don't fret. There are millions of entrepreneurs who have built successful businesses without an MBA. Nevertheless, they were committed to learning entrepreneurial skills through other avenues, such as reading business books, attending workshops, or taking short online courses.

To improve your chances of success, you will need to continuously upgrade your skill set by acquiring both hard and soft skills. Hard skills are the analytical or technical skills that help you manage your growing business, while soft skills are the interpersonal skills that help you build stronger business relationships. Below is a combination of hard and soft skills that you will need to continuously improve at as a leader:

1. Business Management

One of the basic skills you will need to learn and develop is business management. As a leader, you are responsible for managing the day-to-day operations of your business and putting in place processes that help your business grow. Business management skills can help you create dynamic business strategies and find ways to make your business more profitable and manage your growing team.

2. Leadership

Leadership skills can make business management more effective since being a leader is more than just having a likable personality. You need to know how to communicate with your team, so you can provide mentorship and help them thrive in their respective roles. Leadership skills can also help you set a vision and culture for your business and ensure your team is motivated to succeed.

3. Communication

You set the tone when it comes to the amount of openness and transparency you achieve internally (with your employees) and externally (with the customers you serve). When you have excellent communication skills, everybody, on all levels of your business, understands what is expected of them. Good communication skills also help you translate your vision into your brand and on marketing material so that you can reach the ideal target audience.

4. Customer Service

Your customers are the lifeline of your business. Without them, your business cannot grow. Each customer is different and desires to be treated with care and consideration when interacting with your business. Having customer service skills can help you develop a customer-centric business where every process or system within your business prioritizes the needs of the customer. You can also master the art of cold calling, email marketing, and dealing with disgruntled customers online or over the phone.

5. Finance

Every entrepreneur must have basic financial literacy so that they can manage their business funds, create financial forecasts, create invoices, and find ways to maximize their profits. Thankfully, start-up businesses can use bookkeeping software to manage their financial records; however, entrepreneurs will still need to understand how to read and analyze financial statements, as well as how to file tax returns.

6. Critical Thinking

Critical thinking is the ability to rationalize ideas and seek logical evidence when making arguments or problem-solving. As an entrepreneur, it's important to learn how to analyze information from multiple perspectives, so you can develop rich business strategies that take into consideration many factors and provide the best solutions.

7. Time Management

Every plan or strategy that you implement must have a specific deadline. This deadline ensures that work is done at a reasonable pace to achieve your business objectives. Without deadlines, you won't be able to make certain projections or work toward growing your business. Time management skills help you organize your time, so you can complete your tasks within the time frame you have set. They can also help you work more efficiently as a business and keep up with market demands.

WHY CURIOSITY IS YOUR BEST TRAIT

Curiosity is often seen as a disruptive element in a business because it questions existing processes and assesses whether they are effective in achieving business objectives. Entrepreneurs are usually too afraid to question their processes because, as the saying goes, "If it's not broken, you don't need to fix it." However, waiting until something bad happens before assessing your plans and processes is a recipe for disaster.

The definition of curiosity is having a desire to learn something. An entrepreneur who is curious seeks to first understand "why" behind their decisions before considering the "what." For example, after the first six months of your business, you might decide that you want to lease an office space where you can operate your business from, but if you are naturally curious, you will first consider why you want to lease an office space in the first place. Is it because your operations have expanded and you can no longer run your business from your garage, or do you feel the pressure to work from an office space because that's what most successful entrepreneurs do? By going deeper and looking into your decision, you are able to learn more about your motivations, which could end up saving you a lot of money!

Curiosity is also beneficial for another reason: It can help you challenge your ideas. Now, you might be wondering why you would want to challenge your ideas. Think about this way: Before smartphones came to exist, we had to purchase digital cameras to take high-quality photos, manually write down our to-do lists, and buy physical copies of books. This single innovation allowed us to organize various aspects of our lives on one device. Without seeking to challenge the status quo and look beyond conventional wisdom, businesses wouldn't be able to modernize industries and change how ordinary people live.

Steve Jobs is a good example of a leader who continuously challenged his ideas, and as a result, he was able to create products that changed how people communicate and interact with technology. In 2007, after successfully releasing the Macintosh computer and the iPod, Steve Jobs introduced his latest product, which combined three revolutionary products in one device:

Well today we're introducing three revolutionary products of this class. The first one is a widescreen iPod with touch controls, the second is a revolutionary mobile phone, and the third is a breakthrough internet communications device. So three things: a widescreen iPod with touch controls, a revolutionary mobile phone, and a breakthrough internet communications device. These are not separate devices. This is one device. And we are calling it iPhone. (Guglielmo, 2017)

The iPhone not only solved a communication problem, but it also helped customers identify new needs they didn't even know existed. Who knew that having access to the internet at the touch of a finger, rather than turning on a computer, was what consumers actually wanted? Well, I guess Steve Jobs and his team were curious enough to predict the future technological landscape and how it would change communication forever.

Curiosity is your greatest weapon because it allows you to ask questions that lead to innovative solutions, which ultimately improve your business processes. Instead of settling for what you know or how things move in your industry, you can find ways to combine unrelated ideas or borrow techniques from other industries to upgrade your products and services. Staying curious can also help you make intentional decisions. Before completing a task, you can ask yourself if it's worth the time and money it takes to complete it or whether it can help you meet your short-term goals.

Here are a few business improvement questions you can ask yourself or your team to help you push beyond your current boundaries and think outside the box:

1. What is the one thing standing in the way of generating more revenue? How can you improve your current processes to make your business more profitable?
2. What are some of the new market opportunities you can look into? Are there any business strategies you can implement to increase the market share of your business?
3. What is the one thing your customers need that they are not aware of yet? How can you improve your products or services to address this unconscious need?
4. How can you get more customers without increasing your marketing budget? How can you sell more products without launching new products?
5. Which internal processes need to be revamped? How can you use technology to make your processes more agile?

LESSON 5: READY, FIRE, AIM!

Only put off until tomorrow what you are willing to die having left undone.
—Pablo Picasso

THERE IS NO PERFECT ENTREPRENEUR

An entrepreneur is someone who is analytical and has an eye for detail; however, they are not perfect. They do what is necessary in each moment, but that doesn't mean they make good decisions all of the time. Sometimes, it takes failing and receiving feedback for an entrepreneur to finally find the best solution.

Perfectionism can be defined as an obsessive pursuit of excellence and rejecting anything that appears flawed. An entrepreneur who is also a perfectionist seeks to excel in everything they do and expects the same level of mastery from their employees. The greatest drawback to this is that being a perfectionist makes it hard to pull the trigger and make decisions. The entrepreneur may go back and forth, modifying their plans and overanalyzing their strategies so that it comes out perfect—all of this is done at the cost of speed!

You might disagree with me here, but I believe that speed is more important than a perfect outcome. Entrepreneurs are often advised to "fail quickly" so that they can find new solutions without wasting much time. When you are seeking a perfect outcome, you spend far too much time refining a plan and not enough time testing it out. What happens when the plan doesn't yield the outcomes you desire? Can you somehow get a refund on the precious time you wasted?

A perfectionist entrepreneur is constantly busy working at something, but that doesn't mean they are productive. Some of the challenges they may face when running their business are time delays, missed deadlines, unfulfilled commitments, and budget overruns. They may also expect those working underneath them to have the same desire for excellence and achieve unrealistic performance standards. Since no one is perfect, employees can become discouraged working in a high-performance environment with very little praise or appreciation for the work they do.

Start-up businesses today are faced with new challenges, like competing in a digital world. What makes start-ups competitive nowadays is the speed of responding to customers and the delivery of services. For example, it's highly unlikely that a customer will notice a perfect sales pitch from a decent one, but guess what? If you take too long to respond to their calls or follow up after an inquiry, that is something they may remember for the rest of their life.

As an entrepreneur, your aim shouldn't be perfection because perfection is an illusion. Instead, your aim should be to learn how to assess risks, make decisions in the shortest amount of time, and create a crisis management plan, so you can quickly bounce back after a poorly executed plan or strategy.

High Expectations vs. Unrealistic Expectations

Here's the question of the century: What is the difference between having high expectations and having unrealistic expectations? Surely, if the aim of businesses is to compete in highly competitive markets, shouldn't entrepreneurs set high expectations for their businesses and employees?

Yes, this is true.

High expectations shouldn't be confused with unrealistic standards. Any entrepreneur who desires to improve their leadership skills and business performance will need to set high expectations; otherwise, they may not reach their business goals. Furthermore, if a leader doesn't push employees to work more diligently, then they may get low productivity from their team. In general, when employees know that their leader expects good results from them, then the quality of their work improves. This is known as the Pygmalion effect.

However, there is a thin line between motivating employees to perform better and creating expectations that they will never achieve. For example, when your work expectations are so high that it causes employees to ridicule or resist them, the chances of them meeting these expectations are low. Alternatively, if your employees attempt to meet your high expectations but are constantly met with disapproval from you as their leader, they won't feel motivated to continue pushing themselves that hard. In essence, expectations become unrealistic when they bring down the morale of your employees, challenge the company's integrity, or cause employees to resign or lose respect for the leadership. The effects of unrealistic expectations can also be seen in other factors, such as budget overruns, missing deadlines, high absenteeism, or poor-quality work.

If you want to know how your employees feel about your expectations, the best way to find out is to ask them. Ask your employees if they feel their job tasks are manageable or whether they demand too much out of them. You can also discuss time expectations, like how much time should be allocated for each task or project. Strong and open communication will ensure a bond of trust is built and that your employees feel supported in their roles.

Another way to transfer a good work ethic to your employees is to lead by example. If you set high expectations for yourself as a leader, you can inspire those underneath you to model the same behavior. Good behavior at work is contagious, and when those in positions of authority exhibit a high level of discipline, it can trickle down to those in lower positions, too.

HOW TO FIGHT PROCRASTINATION

Imagine this scenario in your mind: You have 10 unanswered emails from potential business leads that you hope to get to before the end of the week. You noticed that you are out of business supplies. You plan on driving to the other side of town to stock up, but you put this off for later. Your business website is up and running, but you haven't set up your social media profiles as of yet.

This is a clear example of procrastination in action. Procrastination sounds like a lot of "maybe," "soon," or "not yet" and not enough "yes, right now," or "in the next 30 minutes." Just because an entrepreneur has a lot of responsibility on their shoulders doesn't mean they are always proactive in making decisions. In fact, the more tasks, events, and plans an entrepreneur has to think about, the more overwhelmed they might feel to get things done.

Think about the last time you put something really important off. Even when you knew what you were supposed to do and how you were supposed to do it, getting yourself to focus on the task was difficult. You may have even created what sounded like a valid excuse for putting that thing off. For instance, you could've told yourself you don't have enough money, time, or support to get it done. While this may have been true, it wasn't a strong enough reason not to leap forward and take action.

Procrastination is normal for entrepreneurs, especially those transitioning from a nine-to-five job to full-time entrepreneurship. Before, you had a senior manager who would oversee your work and ensure you were meeting your work goals. Now, however, you are your own boss, so it's up to you to hold yourself accountable.

The best approach to fighting procrastination is to have a plan in place, so you can curb it from the onset. But, before you come up with your plan, take a moment to think about the reasons you procrastinate. Here are a few common ones to consider:

- **Procrastinating has become a bad habit.** If procrastinating isn't anything new to you, then it may be a habit you do without even thinking about it. Small habits like not clearing your emails by the end of the day, being productive at the last minute, or avoiding mundane tasks can lead to a lifestyle of procrastination.
- **There are certain tasks about your business that don't excite you.** There is a lot of pressure placed on entrepreneurs to know everything, but quite frankly, it's normal to not find certain aspects of your business, like bookkeeping or creating social media content, particularly interesting. The best approach may be outsourcing these tasks to other firms or automating the majority of the task so that you don't need to spend a lot of time on it.
- **You are overwhelmed with the workload.** Having a lot of work can lead to procrastination. With just thinking

about the many tasks you need to do, you may feel hopeless in completing all of them. When the workload increases, it may be necessary to hire an employee (on a part-time basis at first) who can take on some of the workload.

- **You are indecisive.** You may take a long time to make a decision due to factors like perfectionism or the fear of failure. This can lead to procrastination and overthinking your plans. The danger with indecisiveness is that the longer you delay making decisions, the more afraid you become to take action.

After determining your reason for procrastination, you are now in a better position to come up with a plan to curb procrastination. If procrastination has become a habit, for example, your plan will focus on creating new productive habits, like completing work within the given deadline. Here are a few task management tips that can help you fight procrastination:

- **Rank your daily task in order of importance.** Every task may be important, but not all tasks take priority. Create a to-do list on a daily basis and take a few minutes in the morning to highlight priority tasks. Start with these tasks and do the rest afterward. If you have only managed to complete your priority tasks for the day, consider it a good day!
- **If possible, set short-term deadlines for tasks.** Giving yourself more time to complete a task isn't always the best idea. According to Parkinson's Law, your work expands when there is more time available. For example, if you give yourself two weeks to complete a project, it will take you two weeks to complete it. Thus, your aim

should be to set short deadlines and use the time you have constructively.

- **Use time blocking.** Time blocking is a tool to help you manage your time during the day. On a digital calendar, you can create time blocks, which are time intervals, where you complete certain tasks. In between each time block can be a rest block where you take 10–15 minutes for yourself. During each time block, ensure that your phone is on silent, TV switched off, and additional tabs closed on your laptop.
- **Reward yourself with breaks.** Set a rule for yourself that for every hour you work, you give yourself a 15-minute break. Breaks are important, especially if you are doing tasks where concentration is key. During your break, step away from your screen, drink a glass of water, stretch, meditate, or grab a snack.
- **Focus on single tasks rather than multitasking.** The concept of focusing on multiple tasks at the same time and being productive is a myth. Multitasking is the enemy of productivity and concentration because your mind can only process small quantities of information at once. Instead of flooding your brain with various inputs, choose one task to work on so that you can process and absorb information easily.

THE READY, FIRE, AIM RULE

In the police force, police officers in training are taught to do three things before firing a shot: ready the gun, aim at the target, and then fire the shot. However, to get desired results at the quickest time, Tom Peters and Bob Waterman present a different go-to-market strategy known as the "Ready, Fire, Aim" principle (Peter & Waterman, 2004).

You may be wondering why one would fire before they have aimed at their desired target. The answer is simple: As an entrepreneur, you will never get the perfect aim at your target, so it is better to fire and focus on the aim later. In other words, after you have made a decision, you will receive feedback that can help you refine your next approach until you achieve the desired results. If you wait until you can predict the outcomes, you may miss an opportunity to make a decision. Therefore, in most cases, you have to get comfortable with making a move before you feel ready.

There is another concept in the business world known as paralysis by analysis. In short, this occurs when you spend a lot of time analyzing a decision to the point of being paralyzed, meaning you are hesitant to go ahead with the decision. The creative idea you had just doesn't inspire you anymore, and the enthusiasm you once felt is replaced with skepticism or pessimism. At the end of the day, your action is what counts. You don't get paid for the hours you spend brainstorming, but you could potentially get paid when your ideas are brought to life through skillful action.

So what can you learn from the Ready, Fire, Aim rule? You must get started before you are ready because, let's face it, you will never be fully prepared for the experience of running a business. You need to train yourself to make a decision and think about the impact of your decision afterward. Of course, this doesn't mean you should make bad decisions and suffer the consequences later. You will still need to conduct research and refer to your strategies, so you can make informed decisions. For example, collect 70% of the facts needed to make a decision (this is the getting ready stage), make the decision and move quickly (now you are firing), and then tweak or optimize your plan later (here, you will improve your aim).

A certain guy I knew, who was starting his business at the same time as mine, was what we would call a perfectionist. He got weighed down with the minutiae details involved in creating an e-book that would accompany his products, and by the time he started selling his product, he realized the product was never going to work—he was competing in a saturated market, and the time he spent fussing over his e-book was time completely wasted. The lesson I learned from him was simple: Make quick decisions because there will always be imperfections!

Starting before you are ready isn't about creating vision boards, endless mind maps, or even talking about your business idea. These aren't bad things to do, but when action is required, you need to take a different approach. You need to actually get in your car and visit potential suppliers rather than creating a list of potential suppliers on a spreadsheet. Sign up to workshops if training is what you need. In other words, you have to put in some sweat equity and invest your time and effort into moving yourself from one stage in your business to the next.

If you still feel like something is holding you back, ask yourself these three questions:

1. Do You Need More Information?

If you feel unprepared, chances are you won't feel confident making moves. Remember: The first step in the Ready, Fire, Aim rule is being ready, which means doing the necessary preparations. This could include gathering more research, reports, or surveys to help you make informed decisions. Be careful though: Too much data collection can lead to paralysis by analysis, so set measurable objectives when seeking more information.

2. Do You Need More Experience?

Another hindrance to getting started is not having sufficient knowledge or expertise in the field or industry you are in. To put it lightly, you may be feeling like an amateur and you are afraid of making big decisions that affect your business. Every entrepreneur at some point on their journey has felt like they were inexperienced to make certain decisions for their business, but this shouldn't be a roadblock on your journey. If you need more knowledge about an industry, speak to an expert or enroll in a short course. Better yet, you can earn the experience by learning on the job and learning from every setback. By repeating the same processes over and over again, learning is taking place. This means that whether you are aware of it or not, you are maturing as a leader.

3. Do You Need Support?

Even though it's possible to get started without support, some entrepreneurs may need that extra reassurance or encouragement before they fire. The best place to find support is among close friends and family; however, other sources of support include social groups and clubs, professional platforms like LinkedIn, or from a mentor or coach. Following business discussions online can also be a great way to interact and get encouragement from other start-up entrepreneurs. Remember that you are never alone, and there are groups or online communities of people who are happy to walk this journey with you.

In 1966, a dyslexic teenage kid decided to drop out of high school. One of his friends helped him start a youth magazine, and he made money by selling advertising space in the magazine to local businesses. About four years later, he decided to expand his business by selling mail order records to his customer base of students. This idea was fantastic, and a year later, he had made enough money to open his own record store. Two years into selling records, he made the decision to start his own record label, which had its own recording studio.

Over the next decade, the young man grew his record label and signed bands like Culture Club and The Rolling Stones. On the side, he was starting new businesses like an airline company, fitness club, and a mobile company. To date, there are over 400 different businesses that he has either founded or been a part of. And, despite his inexperience or disability, the young man grew to become a multibillionaire.

Who am I talking about? None other than Sir Richard Branson.

LESSON 6: QUITTING IS NOT AN OPTION

The opposite of quitting is to persevere, just wait a little longer things will turn around soon!

—Dr. Lucas D. Shallua

DON'T BACK DOWN

Jack Ma is the wealthiest man in China, being the founder of the e-commerce giant, Alibaba. His net worth is currently at $36.7 billion, and it continues to grow each year. But, surprisingly, the journey to becoming a billionaire wasn't smooth sailing. Jack Ma faced so much rejection when he was younger that many would've thought he was unlucky, yet he didn't back down.

Coming from the rural parts of China, he didn't grow up being taught English. However, as a teenager, he took it upon himself to learn the universal language. I guess at the back of his mind, he knew that learning English would be a valuable skill in the future. Since he didn't have access to an English teacher or learning material, he visited the Shangri-La hotel each morning and volunteered to take Western tourists on a trip around the city. In exchange for his free tours, he would ask the tourists to teach him a bit of English. He committed to this for nine years and didn't miss a day.

When it came to applying for university, Jack Ma failed his entrance exams three times. He even applied to Harvard and got rejected a total of 10 times. Since universities were not accepting him, he decided to look for work. This too proved unsuccessful. He applied to 30 jobs and was rejected in all of them. One of the jobs he applied to was at a local KFC. About 24 applicants applied to work there, and all of them were accepted—except for Jack Ma. Eventually, Jack Ma got accepted at Hangzhou Normal University and graduated with a bachelor's degree in English. He taught English at a public university in Hangzhou for the next five years before starting Alibaba in 1995.

Can you imagine one of the wealthiest people in the world having such a rough start in life? When we think of successful entrepreneurs, we tend to think they have either had it easy, came from a wealthy family, or were connected with the right people. But the reality is that many entrepreneurs face rejection or have to deal with the odds that are stacked up against them. Jack Ma is proof that rejection is redirection—not the end of the road. Rejection can be the wake-up call you need to try something different or go in a different direction.

Don't back down. Pick yourself up after every setback and try again.

HOW TO KEEP ON KEEPING ON

Perseverance is the ability to stay on course despite the delays or denials you may experience. What better word to describe the journey of entrepreneurship than perseverance? Of course, this doesn't mean that your entire experience being an entrepreneur will be marked with failure or hardship. The highs will be really high, and the lows will be really low. And this is why you need perseverance—to pick yourself up from the low moments and work diligently toward the high moments.

Entrepreneurship is a lot like entering a new relationship with a significant other. During the first few months, you are in the honeymoon phase, and you are passionate about the other person. However, as the months go by, the passion begins to wear off, and you start seeing them for who they are. Your relationship might start feeling bland, as each encounter you have with them feels predictable. If the connection between you isn't strong enough, this is usually when you call it quits. But, if your relationship is built on more than attraction, you will hang in there and develop skills to deal with the highs and lows of the relationship.

Think about your business and where you are in your relationship with it. Are you still in the honeymoon phase, or has the passion fizzled out? If your business is causing you a lot of stress and you feel like quitting each week, remind yourself that every relationship goes through highs and lows. There is no such thing as a fairytale marriage, and there certainly is no such thing as a fairytale business! You need to decide if you're going to call it quits and forget about your business or whether you are going to hang in there and ride the wave. My hope for you is that you keep on keeping on and overcome the hard times you are presented with.

It is rare for any business to succeed on the first try. It takes careful planning, hard work, and the right timing for your business to succeed. However, doing all of this won't guarantee that your business will succeed. In other words, you could spend years doing preparation and long hours each day working hard, but your business may not yield the results you are looking for. Take it from me: There is nothing more painful than sacrificing everything in your power to improve your business and for your sacrifices to go by unnoticed or not make a big enough impact. But, in those moments where I felt like I had given everything and couldn't possibly give anymore, perseverance is what kept me from quitting.

My recent experience of having to persevere was when Brexit was enforced and when COVID-19 bans were announced. Both Brexit and COVID-19 occurred in the same year, and it was catastrophic for my physical products business. From the Brexit policy alone, my business lost tens of thousands of dollars in EU sales for 2021. But that wasn't the end of it. Another $12,000 was lost in credit card hacking and $15,000 lost as a result of "missing shipments." This meant that I needed to order new stock from my supplier, which put us back several thousands of dollars. Yet, through it all, I kept on keeping on—even though at times it felt like I was holding on to the final piece of string. I had to remind myself constantly that I would look back at this experience with pride in how I kept going. Here are three strategies to help you keep going on your journey, as well:

1. Take the Blows

Don't try to avoid challenges because that won't make them disappear. There are some bad situations you are able to anticipate and avoid, and some that creep up behind you and turn your business upside down. The best way to handle crises is to take the blows and don't fight them. It's only when the dust has settled that you can look at what you have left and think about the best way forward. See the challenges you face as a humbling moment and how it will build your character as a leader.

2. Think Success

The worst thing you can do during the lowest points in your entrepreneurial journey is to adopt a defeatist mindset. Even though you are down and out, you don't want to think like someone who is down and out. You cannot stop thinking creatively, strategically, and optimistically when you face trouble. Otherwise, you may never survive what was only meant to be a temporary loss. Read inspirational books, surround yourself with successful people, and work as hard as you would if you were bringing in a lot of revenue.

3. Don't Lose Confidence in Yourself

The first person you will want to blame for your hard times is yourself. You might think that if only you didn't make certain decisions, you wouldn't have ended up in a terrible predicament. But blaming yourself for outcomes that were not in your control won't help you make progress. Even if the mistake was yours, you need to forgive yourself for not making a good business decision. Build your confidence back up by learning the necessary lessons and moving differently going forward. You need to become your own cheerleader and friend so that you can encourage yourself to keep going.

WHAT IS IN YOUR CONTROL?

It can be a bitter pill for any entrepreneur to swallow knowing there are some things outside of their control. As someone with a lot of authority in your business, you are used to having control and overseeing every process. However, every now and then, life does what life knows best and puts you in an unexpected situation that leaves you feeling out of control.

There are certain things within your control and certain things that you can't control—even if you had all of the resources in the world. However, the human tendency is to procrastinate over what you can control and spend hours overthinking what you can't control. I get it: You can't help but obsess over the things that aren't working in your business or the things that are causing you significant stress. The better approach would be to stop thinking about what you can't control and focus instead on the things that are going well. But how many times do you actually do this?

Stephen Covey, in his book titled, *The 7 Habits of Highly Effective People,* suggests that every person has a circle of concern and a circle of influence (Covey, n.d.) The circle of concern includes all of the things you care about but don't have control over. This includes the economy, your family, and illness. The circle of influence includes all of the things that you care about and can positively impact. This circle includes factors like your time, goals, effort, and mindset. To persevere during tough times, you would need to focus on the things within your circle of influence rather than ruminating on the things that you care about but can't control.

For example, since you can't control the economy, why stress about it? Don't get me wrong; it's important to care about what is happening in your country and how it could potentially affect your business. However, you are better off restructuring your business to adapt to the changes in the economy because at least that is within your control. The same goes for personal issues you may face, like illness. As scary as the thought may be of getting sick, there is no point spending time worrying about getting sick. Instead, you can redirect that energy on improving your eating habits, getting active, and spending as much time on things that bring you joy.

With all this being said, you have two options on how to deal with unexpected circumstances: You can either be proactive or reactive. The proactive approach would be to spend the majority of your time and energy focusing on what you can positively change in your life. Even in the worst of scenarios, this will give you a sense of control and help you remain resilient. Alternatively, you can take the reactive approach and focus on the things that concern you, but you can't change. Doing this will make you feel like your challenges are insurmountable, and you will find it very difficult to endure. The choice is yours. What will it be: a proactive or reactive approach?

The One Thing You Can Control

There are many factors outside of an entrepreneur's control, except one crucial factor—their emotions. You may not be in control of what happens to you, but you have full control of your emotional reaction toward it. Now, this doesn't mean that you should have a positive attitude all of the time. You're human, and sometimes, you will feel frustrated or discouraged. Although, it does mean that you should be careful not to make emotionally charged decisions.

For example, let's consider professionalism in the workplace. You have an opportunity to strike a deal with a supplier you dislike. The deal makes a lot of business sense, but the personality clash between you and the supplier makes you hesitant whether signing the deal is the right decision or not. What do you do? Do you sign the deal because it makes logical sense for your business, or do you turn the deal down because you don't connect well with the supplier?

From a business and professional standpoint, signing the deal would be the right thing to do. However, oftentimes, as leaders, we end up going with decisions that *feel* good to make. Feelings are important when it comes to interpersonal relationships in the workplace, like the relationships you have with your employees. But feelings are misplaced when they become a guiding factor in making strategic business decisions. A decision made out of anger, fear, or guilt doesn't take into account what your business actually needs and what your business objectives are. This is dangerous, and a few of these emotionally charged decisions can change the direction you are heading as a business.

The best way to control your emotions is to become aware of them. When you can feel a strong emotion bubbling up, it should be your cue to stop whatever business-related task you were doing and take a moment to calm yourself down. For example, if you were in the middle of a business discussion and suddenly felt angry because of what someone else said, you could excuse yourself from others and take time to breathe and regain control over your emotions. Responding promptly when you sense a shift in your mood or emotions is the proactive approach to take because it is well within your circle of influence to regulate your emotions.

Being aware of your emotions can also make you aware of your perceptions. For example, when you are in a bad mood, your outlook on your business may be negative, and you might believe that nothing is going right (even though that may not be the case). Your emotions can also cause you to make assumptions about people that are not based on any factual evidence but purely your first impressions of them or whether you feel a connection to them or not. When you are aware of how your emotions affect your opinions, assumptions, and outlook on people, business, and life in general, you can catch yourself whenever you have a strong view about something and assess whether this view is based on facts or your emotions.

Once again, feeling strongly about something isn't bad per se, but allowing those strong feelings to influence your business plans and decisions can have negative consequences. Here are a few coping strategies that you can practice to better control your emotions in your business:

1. Compartmentalize

Trying to keep your personal life separate from your professional life can be a struggle. There may be times when you are so deeply affected by a personal matter that it affects your level of focus, productivity, and decision-making in business. Learning to compartmentalize your feelings can create a clear boundary between work and home. Compartmentalization is the act of separating something into categories. When compartmentalizing your feelings, you train your mind to respond in certain ways around certain environments.

For example, before you start your work day, you can take 10 minutes to meditate and clear your mind of personal fears, thoughts, and family issues. If a personal issue arises during the work day, you can do what is known as a "mental lockup," where you mentally arrest the issue and store it in a section of your mind for the time being. The mental lockup also applies at home when you suddenly think of a work-related issue.

2. Breathing Techniques

Regulating your breathing is an effective way of calming your mind and body. When you are feeling strong emotions, your heart rate accelerates, and this causes your breathing rate to increase. When you are breathing heavily, you can trigger your body's natural stress response and feel anxious. By focusing on your breathing and deliberating, slowing it down, and getting back into a normal rhythm, you can lower your heart rate and reduce stress and anxiety. Below is a simple breathing technique that you can practice at home or at work:

- Take a deep breath through your nose and count to four slowly
- Hold your breath for two counts
- Gently release the breath of your mouth, counting to four slowly again

- While breathing, you can think of an emotional situation or negative thought that you want to release from your mind. When you exhale, imagine that you are releasing this emotional situation or negative thought out of your body.

3. Seek Clarity

When you are emotional, your rational brain shuts down. This means that most of what you are feeling may be inflated and not an accurate representation of what is happening in your environment. Before reacting, seek to understand the context of the situation by looking at it from multiple perspectives and asking questions. Challenge your own perceptions by finding other narratives to explain the situation. For example, instead of thinking that someone is deliberately sabotaging you, consider whether it might have been a miscommunication on your part.

4. Understand Your Emotional Triggers

Emotional triggers are the words, thoughts, or behaviors that cause you to lose your cool. Most times, you can trace your emotional triggers back to past events in your life where you felt angry, taken for granted, lonely, or betrayed. When you are reminded of the painful event, you react negatively. Understanding your triggers can help you avoid certain people, places, or things that could potentially upset you. For example, you might find yourself getting frustrated whenever you are around an arrogant person, so you try by all means to avoid arrogant people. If avoiding your triggers isn't possible, finding ways to tune out of what's going on around you and tune into what is happening within you can help you feel less defensive and plan how you are going to navigate the triggering situation in a healthy and professional way.

5. Create Standards

To control your emotions at work, you can set rules that govern how you and your employees respond when you are feeling emotional. For example, you can introduce pause breaks where employees can take around 10 minutes away from their desk to calm down, stretch their legs, and regain focus. You can also create a culture where employees are encouraged to seek clarity before allowing their emotions to cloud their judgment or hold off communicating with stakeholders when they are feeling emotional.

LESSON 7: DON'T FEAR HARD WORK

The only place where success comes before work is in the dictionary.
—Vidal Sassoon

WHAT WORKING HARD LOOKS LIKE

The CEO of Apple starts his work day at 4:30 a.m. The owner of the Dallas Mavericks, Mark Cuban, didn't go on vacation for seven years while starting up his business. Facebook's COO, Sheryl Sandberg, has been said to leave work at 5:30 p.m. to eat dinner with her children and then get back to work after she has put her children to sleep.

What do these successful leaders have in common? An incredible work ethic.

I was speaking to a friend of mine many years ago about the journey start-up entrepreneurs take to build successful businesses. My friend was a seasoned entrepreneur at the time, so he decided to share a lesson he learned during the early stages of his business. He said, "I had to take a hard look at myself and decide whether I wanted short-term gratification or long-term bliss."

I have held on to this lesson throughout my business journey and often check in with myself to assess my intentions. There was no excuse I could make for not working hard. I had big dreams—the kind of dreams that require a lot of manpower! So I knew that hard work was going to be a major theme in my life. However, the question of short-term gratification or long-term bliss helped me find the motivation for working hard. Quite frankly, I knew that short-term gratification would mean making a few extra hundred dollars a month and living a comfortable life. But I didn't want a comfortable life; I wanted an extraordinary life! I was aiming for long-term bliss, and that required an extreme work ethic to achieve.

Don't be fooled by those that claim to have overnight success or the get-rich-quick crew—real and long-lasting wealth is accumulated over time through consistent work. And what about the sacrifices entrepreneurs have to make? Well, those are billed separately. The daily sacrifices made to run a business don't replace the amount of work entrepreneurs invest. In other words, even after you have given your time and money, you cannot hold off on the effort you put in your business.

If this explanation of the kind of work ethic you need as a start-up entrepreneur isn't making you afraid, then you, my friend, have what it takes to succeed at this game. People who are not entrepreneurs might look at your daily routine and think you are crazy for investing as much as you do into their business. After all, only a few people would start their day before 8 a.m. or work until the late hours of the night. However, since entrepreneurship is what gives you a sense of purpose, you are willing to adjust to the demands of your business and create a lifestyle that supports your business goals.

How Hard Is Hard?

You might be asking yourself the question: *How hard is hard?*

Before we answer that question, perhaps we should distinguish between work ethic and hard work. Work ethic can be defined as the set of moral values and expectations you have around your work. People with a good work ethic tend to have excellent time management, organization, and planning skills. They know how to structure their day so that they can maximize their productivity and achieve their daily goals.

Then, what is hard work? Is hard work described in the traditional sense where you need to do things manually? Is it about the number of hours you put into your business each week, or can hard work be more about working smart and using technology to increase your speed and efficiency?

First and foremost, let's speak about the hours of work you put into your business each week. Every entrepreneur has their own style of working. For example, some entrepreneurs are early risers and prefer to get a good portion of work done before their day gets busy. Other entrepreneurs are night owls and would rather sleep in the early hours of the morning to catch up on the day's work. The amount of hours entrepreneurs invest each week also varies, with some entrepreneurs being comfortable putting in about 60 hours of work each week. However, the time of day you choose to work and the amount of hours you put in is only an indication of work ethic—not necessarily a display of how hard you work.

Hard work is the total amount of energy and effort you spend laboring on tasks. Unlike work ethic that considers values and expectations, hard work only looks at the physical investment you make in achieving your goals. This means that the time of day you work or the amount of hours you put in doesn't necessarily make you a hard worker. For instance, sitting on the couch for 10 hours each day browsing the internet doesn't make you a hard worker because there is barely any physical exertion happening. Hard work is all about being productive, like driving from A to B, picking up the phone, typing an email, refining your business strategy, having meetings with potential partners, and so on.

Here are a few strategies that can help you work harder, while maintaining your excellent work ethic:

1. Practice the 80/20 Rule

The 80/20 rule suggests that 80% of your results come from 20% of your daily activities. In other words, if you had a list of 10 tasks to complete in a day, only two of those tasks generate the kind of impact or results you need to move forward. Of course, this doesn't make the other eight tasks meaningless, but it does mean that you would need to spend the majority of your energy on your most important tasks. You can also apply the 80/20 rule in your business so you can see where you need to invest most of your energy. For example, 20% of your customers bring in 80% of your revenue. Therefore, these would be the customers you spend a lot of time making happy!

2. Avoid Being Busy

Being busy is never a good thing because it could mean a lot of things. You could be busy being distracted, busy overthinking, or busy on the wrong set of tasks. You should aim to be productive because at least productivity is measurable. Since you will have a lot of responsibility on your shoulders, there will be many issues that aren't real issues or many tasks that don't take priority. When you are thinking about something or working on a task, stop for a moment and assess whether you are busy or productive. When you have free time and are looking for something to do, ask yourself: *What small thing can I do that will make a big impact on my business?*

3. Delegate Work

Just because working hard requires you to exert energy doesn't mean you have to do everything by yourself. Overwhelming yourself with work isn't smart because it can eventually reduce your level of productivity. If you find it difficult to cope with the amount of work you have, delegate work to other people. Look for business tasks that require a lot of concentration and technical, analytical, or creative ability. Delegate these tasks to your staff or outsourced workers, so you can reduce your workload.

When Working Hard Is Unhealthy

Sometimes, you'll need to burn the candle at both ends for a short time, but you shouldn't let extreme hard work drift into the long term. I'll be honest: When I started my entrepreneurial journey, I had an insane work ethic plus worked incredibly hard. At the time, I was still working a nine-to-five job, so I had to find a way to juggle going to work from 8 a.m. to 4 p.m. and invest time into my business. This meant that I worked mornings, evenings, and weekends if I had to in order to get my new business idea off the ground. I did this for three years straight, and it paid off!

Eventually, I had to adjust the amount of time and work I put into my business so that I wouldn't reach burnout. I knew that if working hard came at the expense of my mental and physical health, then it wouldn't help me remain sustainable in the long term. Yes, in the first few years when I didn't have many employees and did most of the work by myself (with the help of my family), working extreme hours wasn't an option. But, when my systems had been put in place and I could afford to hire more people, I could take a step back.

Doing anything to the extreme is not advisable. In the short term, you might make a lot of progress, but after a while, you will grow weary, lose focus, and feel physically exhausted. Your health and well-being as an entrepreneur is vital to the success of your business—in fact, it's more important than making profits. It's common for entrepreneurs to not take any leave, even when they are sick, but here are a few signs that you may be due for a vacation or at least time away from work:

- **You're not getting the same results as you used to.** You are working with the same intensity as you have been for many months or years, but you aren't getting the same trusted results. In other words, your output doesn't match your input. This can be a sign that you aren't working efficiently anymore, which could be a result of a lack of focus or fatigue.
- **You have lost a passion for your business.** Running your business used to be fun. Now, it feels like a strenuous job full of the same routines (a lot like how you felt when you had a normal day job). You aren't excited to go to work in the morning or think of new ways to grow your business. Taking a break can revive the love for what you do and make you motivated to succeed again.
- **You have trouble focusing.** Common signs of burnout are a lack of concentration and poor working memory. At work, you may be forgetful, struggle to meet your deadlines, or find it hard to produce quality work or make quality decisions. If you can't remember simple tasks or don't have the mental energy to think critically

about decisions, then you may be taking on too much work.

- **You struggle to fall asleep at night.** Your sleeping patterns have become irregular, and you spend most of the night wide awake. In the mornings, you wake up feeling grumpy and tired from having too little sleep. Having sleep troubles is a sign that there is a lot on your mind. You may be dealing with a lot of stressful situations or feeling anxious about the state of your business. Taking a break from work can help you calm your mind and properly sort through the problems you are facing. During this break, it may also be useful to see a therapist who can help you manage your stress better.
- **You find yourself spending too much time browsing the internet.** Another sign that you are probably overworked is mindlessly surfing the internet or your social media feed. Social media, like any addiction, has a numbing effect on the brain. It can provide you with an escape from the real world, so you don't have to think about your current circumstances. Eventually, this could lead to feelings of burnout, depression, or lack of interest in your work.
- **You don't have a social life.** The work-life balance is crucial because it protects you from things like burnout. Your business is important, but at the end of the day, it is what you do—not who you are. If you don't have a life outside of your business, it's probably time to take a break and find side interests, hobbies, and social groups to be a part of.
- **Your physical health is declining.** If you notice that you tend to get sick more often, it may be a sign that you are overworking yourself. When you don't give your body sufficient rest, your immune system can weaken,

> which makes you vulnerable to sickness. Common physical symptoms to look out for are irregular sleeping patterns, gut issues, chronic migraines, unexplained mood swings, chronic fatigue, and colds.

Your body needs to be given the right fuel so that it can sustain itself. When you are only getting three hours of sleep at night, eating highly processed foods during the day, and returning to sit on your couch in the evenings, then you will experience health problems. The success of your business rests on the quality of your well-being. Thus, don't overwork yourself to the point of compromising your health.

SWITCHING FROM AN EMPLOYEE TO EMPLOYER MINDSET

Entrepreneurs tend to pride themselves in working hard. Why? Well, the harder they work, the closer they get to achieving their goals and proving that all of the risks, sacrifices, and tears were worth it. An employee won't look at hard work in the same way because they are not expected to work longer than what their contract stipulates. Moreover, they aren't responsible for managing the team or overseeing any tasks other than their own work. Therefore, when making a transition from your day job to entrepreneurship, it's important to undergo a mindset shift.

How you processed information, solved problems, structured your day, or planned your career advancement as an employee will be different when you become an entrepreneur. The circumstances you will have to deal with will require a different type of thinking as well as a different type of work ethic. For example, you can't wait for things to happen. You are responsible for making things happen. If you are going to decide to not go to work, then no work will be done. There needs to be a sense of urgency in how you move and make decisions; otherwise, you might miss out on golden business opportunities.

As an entrepreneur, you also need to simultaneously work on your short- and long-term goals. In most cases, employees only need to focus on their short-term goals and leave the long-term strategies and vision to their managers. However, you are the manager now, and you need to know where you are taking your business and the steps for getting there. You must also come to terms with the fact that what you fail to do today will impact how your tomorrow looks. Therefore, how you manage the time you have now will shape how your business performs in six months or a year.

Do you remember your comfort zone? Yeah, you kissed that place goodbye when you decided to become an entrepreneur. Out of everybody in your team, you are the one who is willing to take most of the risks, test out new ideas, challenge industry norms, or learn about the latest trends. Through experience, you have learned how to have thick skin and continue taking strides in your business despite your setbacks. The upside, however, is that you are free from conformity, meaning you can make your entrepreneurial experience meaningful. You can add your personal quirks to your business and create new norms in your lifestyle.

The switch from an employee to an employer mindset can be overwhelming if you are not prepared for it. If you are still holding on to your day job while running your business, I would suggest starting to make the shift right now. This can give you the enhancement to practice what life as a full-time entrepreneur would look and feel like while still enjoying the comfort of being on someone else's payroll!

As you make the mindset shift from employee to employer, get into the habit of thinking and speaking like an entrepreneur. Here are a few phrases that display the switch in language between an employee and an employer:

1. Mindset on Fear

Employee: “I’m afraid of new challenges that test me beyond my limits.”

Employer: “Fear fuels me to develop my abilities as a leader.”

2. Mindset on Failure

Employee: “Mistakes expose my weaknesses.”

Employer: “Mistakes are feedback that I have taken the wrong approach.”

3. Mindset on Risk

Employee: “Feeling safe means not taking any risk.”

Employer: “Success only comes through taking calculated risks.”

4. Mindset on Knowledge

Employee: “I need to prove that I know it all.”

Employer: “I am continuously learning.”

5. Mindset on Networking

Employee: “I need to be the smartest person in any given room.”

Employer: “I surround myself with people who are more talented and successful than I am, so I can learn something from them.”

6. Mindset on Hard Work

Employee: "I will only work as much as I get paid."

Employer: "I need to invest a lot of work now, so I can take a back seat later."

LESSON 8: PUT YOUR STRENGTHS TO WORK

Your talent determines what you can do. Your motivation determines how much you are willing to do. Your attitude determines how well you do it.
—Lou Holtz

HOW TO IDENTIFY YOUR STRENGTHS

When you analyze your competitors, you look for their strengths and weaknesses. These are the things that show you what your competitors are good at and the competitive advantage you could potentially have on them. However, your business will also have its own set of strengths and weaknesses—as will you as a leader.

Not every entrepreneur will have the same set of strengths and weaknesses. This is evident in the different kinds of innovative ideas, business processes, and company cultures that exist. Success in business has a lot to do with finding what makes you unique as an entrepreneur and infusing that "specialness" in how you operate your business.

Your personal strengths are what define you as an individual. In most cases, they will also be the attributes that people remember about you. Your strengths may come as a result of your personality, education, or past experiences. For example, being honest may be a character trait that you exhibited from a young age, but your ability to think critically may be a result of studying a particular degree in university. There are also strengths, like mental toughness, which may have been developed during a difficult time in your life.

The challenge many entrepreneurs face is identifying their strengths and using them for self-improvement and to develop their businesses. Finding your strengths requires a lot of soul-searching and the ability to look at yourself and your life's journey objectively. Here are a few strategies you can use to identify your strengths:

1. Speak to Close Friends and Family

The people who have been in your life for many years have a good idea of who you are and what your strengths could be. Since they have seen you at your worst and your best, you can trust their opinions concerning who you are. Have a discussion with a close friend or family member about some of the major milestones, memories, or challenges you have had in your life. Instead of focusing on the event, look for key strengths that were highlighted in each situation. Bear in mind that they may highlight external strengths since these were what they saw being displayed. You may be in a better position to identify internal strengths that helped you overcome past situations.

2. Make a List of Your Weaknesses

Your weaknesses are your character flaws that are seen during certain situations. Perhaps you get impatient when you are standing in a long queue or get angry in slow-moving traffic. Many times, we try to hide our weaknesses because we believe they undermine who we are, but in reality, being aware of our weaknesses can reveal our hidden strengths. For example, when you are impatient in a long queue, how do you de-escalate the situation? Whatever tactic you use to calm yourself down can point to a strength. Make a list of some personal weaknesses, and next to each weakness, write down the tactic you use to reverse or de-escalate the situation. Look at each tactic and think about the strength it represents. For example, if your tactic is reflecting on your experience, it could show that you have self-awareness, or if you tend to think of Plan B straight after Plan A fails, that could show that you are resilient.

3. Look for Signs of Excitement

When you are working at an activity, pay attention to how you feel while performing it. If what you are doing energizes you or makes you feel grateful, that is a good sign that you are engaging one of your core strengths. For example, a public speaker naturally feels good when they are on a podium because they get to engage one of their core strengths, which is communicating. A chef loses sense of time when he is in the kitchen because he is engaging with his culinary skills. Not every activity will make you feel excited, but those that do are often related to a strength you have.

4. Identify Your Soft Skills

As mentioned earlier, your soft skills are interpersonal skills that you have learned or come naturally to you. These skills can be seen as strengths because they help you build and maintain good relationships in business. Some examples of soft skills include:

- patience
- honesty
- being a good listener
- assertiveness
- fairness

Even though hard skills like coding or financial analysis can give you an advantage when starting your business, your soft skills are what will help you expand your customer base, make new business connections, and build an influential brand.

5. Create a Hypothetical Scenario

Hypothetical scenarios allow you to reflect on your life by placing yourself in different situations and seeing how you would respond to them. Think of a hypothetical scenario in your head where you are required to use one of your strengths. You might be in a team with two other people, and each of you needs to carry out a task. Consider the task that would come naturally to you or one you would volunteer to do for free. Next, think about which aspect of the project you would spend most of your time working on. Would it be the brainstorming, strategy, interacting with customers, or leadership? You may find that there is more than one aspect of the project you enjoy, and that is also okay.

I remember when I was still working my day job, I picked up Marcus Buckingham's book, *Go Put Your Strengths to Work* (Buckingham, 2010). In the book, he teaches readers how to optimize their strengths and create a life that feels meaningful. For Marcus Buckingham, strengths have little to do with what you are good at but more so what energizes you. One of the exercises in the book requires two different colored post-it notes. In one color, let's say the yellow post-it note, you write down the tasks you enjoy doing during the week. These could be work-related or leisure tasks. In the other color, let's say pink sticky note, you write down your least favorite tasks that you do on a weekly basis. A good way to distinguish between your favorite and least favorite tasks is to ask yourself two questions:

- What do I do during the week that makes me lose track of time?
- What do I do during the week that makes me drag my feet?

I followed the exercise and created two piles of sticky notes: one for my favorite tasks and the other for my least favorite tasks. Next, I sorted each pile into themes and came up with my top three loves and my top three hates. After doing this exercise, I received a lot of clarity regarding my strengths. It made me realize I was in the wrong job, and within months, I had left my job to start my first business!

TOP QUALITIES OF MODERN ENTREPRENEURS

The business landscape has changed since the early 2000s. One of the reasons for the changes in how businesses are run has to do with the rise in technological advancements and how this has made speed a crucial element in everyday business. Modern entrepreneurs are faced with unique problems that require quick problem-solving and dynamic solutions. So what kinds of qualities can ensure entrepreneurs remain competitive in this fast-paced environment? Here are four qualities that make a modern entrepreneur successful:

1. Resilience

Resilience is the ability to bounce back from hardships as

quickly as possible. Every entrepreneur gets caught up in situations that bring them down, but resilient entrepreneurs refuse to stay down. They are also confident in making tough decisions that other people would be afraid to make because they look at the value behind the decision—not the short-term discomfort it may cause.

Tips for developing resilience: Don't let your crises define who you are. See each crisis as a speed bump, not a mountain, which you can overcome. Part of being resilient is also maintaining a positive perception of yourself and your ability to succeed. Remind yourself that your goals are achievable if you put one foot in front of the other.

2. Having a Clear Vision

When an entrepreneur has a clear vision, they know exactly where they are going and the steps they need to take to get there. They are also able to communicate their vision to the rest of their team so that, as a unit, they move in the same direction. Another component of having a clear vision is knowing when to refine or adjust it so that the business can compete in the market and remain relevant in the industry.

Tips for creating a clear vision: When setting a clear vision, it's encouraged to dream big. Create an ideal in your mind that you would love your business to achieve one day. Thereafter, work backward and consider the various big and small goals you will need to accomplish to realize your vision. Note that your vision doesn't necessarily have to be concrete. It can be an abstract idea or dream that you have for your business. However, your goals must be concrete, measurable, and time-bound.

3. Customer-Centered

Being customer-centered means putting the customer at the core of a business. Companies that value customers consider them in every process and strategy that is implemented. A customer-centered entrepreneur will often have good people and communication skills, and the compassion they have for their customers will influence how they run their business and treat their employees. In general, customer-centered entrepreneurs create diverse and positive work cultures.

Tips for becoming more customer-centered: From the top-level manager to the lowest worker, instill a sense of empathy for the customer. It's not enough to say, "The customer is always right" because that statement isn't accurate, and it doesn't truly seek to understand the customer's experience. Showing your customers empathy is about understanding how your product or service improves their lives and making the journey from purchasing a product to receiving it as seamless as possible.

4. Upholding Values

The greatest test of character is seeing how an entrepreneur behaves under pressure. For example, there are two ways of getting capital when you are desperate: find fraudulent ways of getting money or make self-sacrifices. Sometimes, the idea of success and making a lot of money can be so enticing that entrepreneurs compromise their values on the way to the top. But entrepreneurs who value integrity over money, status, or success are able to build their businesses organically and achieve long-term success and sustainability.

Tips for upholding your values: Perhaps the oldest and truest advice for upholding your values is learning to say no to the free lunch. Nothing in life comes free, and this includes business favors or business opportunities. Be careful who you associate yourself with and what you agree to do to get to the top. You might think that compromising on your principles is harmless, but after you have shown yourself that there are certain things you are willing to do for money, you will come across people who are willing to offer you more money if you continue to compromise yourself.

RECRUITING THE DREAM TEAM THAT WILL TAKE YOU TO THE TOP

As an individual, you are creative, intelligent, and passionate about your business. However, very soon, you won't be able to run your business on your own. You will need to recruit your own team of staff who have similar strengths as you and translate your vision into a reality!

The global job market has undergone major transformation over the past few years. Yes, you guessed it, most of the transformation is triggered by the evolving digital landscape. Jobs that human beings used to perform are now performed by machines, and new skills that can help businesses adapt to the times are in demand. However, in America, a new trend known as the "Great Resignation" is ensuing amid the pandemic. According to the U.S. Bureau of Labor Statistics, about four million Americans quit their jobs in July of 2021 (U.S. Bureau of Labor Statistics, 2022). Some of the reasons for this voluntary resignation include low job satisfaction, the refusal to return to work after working remotely, and stagnant wages.

As an entrepreneur looking for talented people to join your dream team, this is good news for you! The market is full of job seekers, many of whom are open to a career change or trying out a new position, so you have a good pool of talent to choose from. However, not every talented person is necessarily a good fit for your business. Similar to how there are desirable traits for entrepreneurs, there are also desirable traits for start-up employees. Here are some of the strengths you should look for in your next hire:

- **Resourcefulness:** You need people who are great problem-solvers and look for ways to simplify processes. This quality is crucial because your start-up business won't have a lot of money to play with, so the most cost-effective and simplest ideas are required.
- **Tenacity:** If you as an entrepreneur have the spirit of never giving up, your employees need to carry the same spirit, too. Look for people who have a generally positive outlook on life and aren't afraid of new challenges. You need people who won't be afraid to make mistakes because that is usually where learning takes place.
- **Creativity:** Even if creativity isn't one of the top skills you are looking for, your dream team must consist of a few creative people who question existing norms, look for new ways to solve existing problems, and have different viewpoints to share. In the modern world, innovation will continue to be one of the defining factors of industry leading businesses since there is a constant demand for new and tech-savvy products and services.
- **Willingness to learn:** The skills and qualifications your employees come with when they join your company will become outdated within three to five years. Research has shown that skills have a life span of five years, although technical skills have a life span of just 2.5 years (Malik, 2020). This means that your employees need to have a passion for learning and improving their skill sets.
- **Teamwork:** Your start-up will face many challenges in the first few years that require your employees to collaborate and solve problems as a team. Good

teamwork involves knowing when and how to communicate with others; delegate tasks and roles; and being open to learn from others.

One of the factors that could make job seekers hesitant to apply to work for your company is the fact that you are still growing. You may not be able to provide the same kind of security they had when they were working for an already established company. However, there are some benefits you can offer your employees to respond to their work needs and make them excited to join your dream team. For example, you could offer alternative benefits that appeal to their lifestyle, such as coverage for pet insurance if you are hiring pet lovers or unlimited vacation days if you are offering a remote position. If you are recruiting young people, offering mentorship or career development opportunities or helping them pay off student debt can be great benefits to offer. Remember that not all benefits need to have a cost attached to them. Some benefits, like having flexible clothing guidelines, won't cost you a cent.

You should also consider modern work preferences, such as part-time or remote working styles. Although, remote work isn't suitable for every company. For instance, there may be certain tasks that your employees need to do in the office because all of your files, stock, and equipment are kept at the office. Offering remote work can also be expensive if you are looking to provide internet adapters to your employees, so they can access the internet. Furthermore, if your business pays per hour, it can be difficult to measure how many hours your employees spend working when they don't have to clock in and out. Do your research and see whether these kinds of modern working arrangements would work for your business.

LESSON 9: AVOID DIGITAL DISTRACTIONS

In the age of technology there is constant access to vast amounts of information. The basket overflows; people get overwhelmed; the eye of the storm is not so much what goes on in the world, it is the confusion of how to think, feel, digest, and react to what goes on.

—Criss Jami

THE GOOD AND THE UGLY OF TECHNOLOGY

We've spoken a lot about technology throughout the book. That alone should tell you just how important it is to the success of your business. As much as you will compete against other businesses in your industry, you will also need to keep up with the ever-changing nature of technology.

Without a doubt, you will need technology to power your business. Even if your business doesn't operate online, you will need an online presence as well as digital software to make running your business easier. Nevertheless, at some point, you will need to draw the line and determine when you are spending too much time on technology.

Technology isn't all bad, but it isn't all good either. First, let's consider the benefits of using technology. I think you can agree that technology has made it more convenient to connect with friends and family, customers, and business partners from around the world. With innovations like video conferencing, you can set up a virtual meeting or group chat and get to speak with anybody in the world in real time. Flexible communication has also allowed for new business industries, like e-commerce, to gain popularity. Instead of being limited by a brick-and-mortar store, you can trade 24 hours a day and have customers who live in different continents.

Technology has also made it easier for businesses to transact. Do you remember the checkbook? If you're a young entrepreneur, you may not know what I'm referring to. Payments are no longer done manually by writing a check or going inside a bank to deposit cash. Consumers can pay for their transactions online, using payment platforms, tap-to-pay features, wire transfers, and other card-free options. This is an advantage for businesses because it means that there are less barriers getting in the way to make sales.

As an entrepreneur who is dedicated to continuous learning, technology makes it easier for you to complete courses, training programs, or read books—all without attending an educational institution. In fact, online learning is in such great demand that the global e-learning market is valued at $101 billion (Statista, 2022). The ability to complete degrees, watch informative seminars, or attend online workshops from the comfort of your home is what continues to make the internet one of the best places to source information.

However, as mentioned earlier, technology is not all good. Being excessively connected to technology can create dependency. Technology dependency occurs when you cannot carry out your daily routine successfully without relying on technology. Of course, you might need to check on your emails once a day, create invoices, or call customers. But, if you can't spend a few hours away from your mobile device, laptop, or headphones, then it may be a sign of technology dependency.

The convenience offered by technology is both a blessing and a curse. We have already discussed how it can be a blessing, but let's look deeper at how it can also be a curse. When you make a habit of being connected to people online, it can make you disillusioned about your reality. The online world tends to be an exaggerated and morphed depiction of the real world. Just take a look at the headlines on news sites or the conversations that take place on social media and reflect on your lived reality. The media has a way of sensationalizing news, current affairs, and the lifestyles of the rich and famous to the extent that it makes you feel dissatisfied and disconnected with your own life.

This feeling of disillusionment can lead to self-esteem issues as well as mental illness. Think about it: How would you feel if you exposed yourself to a fantasy life each day, for many years, and had to justify why your real life doesn't look that way? Besides changing how you look at yourself and your life, technology can also make everyday experiences feel meaningless. For instance, why would you make time to have a face-to-face meeting with a client when you can schedule a Zoom call? Why would you need to take a walk outside when you can put on your headphones and listen to nature music?

The more disconnected you become to everyday life experiences, the less happiness you experience in your life. You are a human being, and your natural human instinct and human needs haven't gone away. Being in the sun still makes you feel more positive and so does catching up with friends and family in person! Getting outside of the house may still be banned in some parts of the world, but even having real plant life or eating fresh foods is still enough to make you feel whole.

The sad truth is that unless you draw boundaries between the use of technology for business purposes and the use of technology for social reasons, you will feel overwhelmed and burned out from excessive technology usage. There is a space and time for technology; however, it doesn't need to invade every aspect of your life. It's also important to know when too much technology usage is negatively impacting your health and the measures to put in place to protect your well-being.

SIGNS THAT YOU ARE DEPENDENT ON TECHNOLOGY

Would you say that you are dependent on technology? You may not realize it, but technology is addictive. From the tap of a finger, you can gain access to any kind of information you want. With so much access, it can be difficult to control how much technology you use and when it's healthy to move away from your screen.

Even though it's still possible to live a tech-free, private life, very few people choose to follow this path. It's like telling a kid in a candy store to refrain from buying candy—it's nearly impossible! But perhaps living a tech-free private life is something you should at least strive for because it can drastically improve your mental and physical health and make you feel more connected to your life. If you are still wondering whether you are dependent on technology, here are a few signs that you can look for:

1. Not Being Online Makes You Anxious

Whenever your phone is switched off or you need to put it on silent for a few hours, you feel anxious. You can't bear the thought of being unreachable to whoever may want to contact you. You may even experience a panic attack when you can't find your phone or when you have missed an important call.

2. You Schedule Time Online

You would much rather carry over certain tasks to the following day than miss a show on TV or skip your favorite podcast. Even though most shows online are either repeated or available for download, you insist on binging on your shows and never missing an episode. Sacrificing your time to be online means that some of your important tasks (the 20% daily tasks that generate 80% of results) take a back seat or aren't seen as being urgent.

3. You Have Forgotten How to Communicate

Since technology isn't interactive (most of the time, you are looking at a white screen), you may forget some of your interpersonal skills, like communicating with people. You could also be confused on what to speak about, especially if you spend most of your time online reading tabloids and following clickbait articles. The best way to practice your communication skills is to have frequent in-person exchanges. This is difficult when most of your exchanges are via text, email, or group chats.

4. You Overwork Yourself

Technology dependency and overworking are linked because tools like email and video conferencing platforms make it easier to continue interacting with your employees and business partners after hours. In fact, you may even be addicted to researching ideas or information online, which counts toward working.

5. You Experience Physical Pain

Your body can also warn you when you have been online for too long. For instance, your eyes can get strained due to the light emitted by your devices; you can get frequent migraines; and if your back is not properly supported, you can also suffer from neck and back pain. It's important to take time a few minutes away from your digital devices every hour or so in order to give your brain and body some much-needed rest.

Benefits of a Digital Detox

Take a moment to think about your average daily routine. Think about how your morning, afternoon, and evening is structured and the typical tasks you do. Now, look back at your routine and count how many times technology features in your day. Do you get woken up by your phone alarm? Do you catch up on current affairs online? What about groceries? Do you buy them using a grocery app?

It has become the norm to integrate technology into everyday life, and this is why a digital detox is necessary. As the name suggests, a digital detox is time spent away from technology for the purposes of resting, reducing distractions, and training yourself to not be so dependent on technology. A digital detox can also be a great way to improve your physical and mental health. For instance, during your detox, you can work on improving your sleeping patterns or spend time journaling.

Similar to a food detox, there are certain things you need to avoid when undertaking a digital detox, such as checking your notifications or emails more than once a day (unfortunately, you can't completely abandon your laptop); playing video games, mindlessly surfing the internet; or watching TV. All of these things may be standard routines that you carry out on a daily basis, hence letting them go won't be easy. Some people, depending on how hooked they are on technology, can experience withdrawal symptoms, like being irritable, restless, anxious, or feeling extremely bored. These withdrawal symptoms are normal, and after a few days, they will go away.

To motivate yourself during a digital detox, keep a reminder of why you have decided to do one in the first place. Were you finding it difficult to meet your work deadlines? Were your intimate relationships with your friends and family suffering? Were you using social media as a form of escapism? Think deeply about the necessity of this detox and how it will improve your personal and professional life.

When you are prepared to do a digital detox, you can follow these steps:

1. Choose One Habit to Change

To make your detox effective, focus on one habit you would like to change. It could be the need to constantly check your notifications or spending hours scrolling through your social media feed. For the rest of your detox, reflect on this habit and start to imagine your life without it.

2. Create a Goal

The next step is to create a goal related to the habit you would like to change. For example, if you desire to stop checking your emails every few minutes, your goal could be to check your emails once a day, preferably during a time you are least busy, like after lunch. If you are always on your social media, you can set a goal to only check social media on certain days of the week, for a specific amount of time. For instance, you can decide to go on social media on Tuesdays from 1 p.m. to 2 p.m. Make your goal specific so you understand what you need to do to achieve it.

3. Set a Time Frame

There are no rules to how short or long your digital detox should be. It's up to you to decide how much time you need to change a harmful habit. Be realistic about how long you can keep up your digital detox, as it does require you to take a break from your digital devices. You can decide to start off light by having a digital detox on a weekend and gradually building up until you can have detoxes that last several weeks or several months. Remember that the aim of each digital detox is to work toward breaking a habit. You may not be able to break it after attempting one detox; it might take you several attempts before you can be completely free from the habit.

4. Reach Out for Support

You can find the detox less overwhelming when you feel encouraged by close friends or family. For instance, ask those living with you to hold you accountable to your detox goal or ask for advice on ways to reduce your dependency on technology. During your detox, it can also be a great time to start new family rituals that don't require technology, such as eating around a dinner table with no cell phones on the table or implementing tech-free zones in your home where anyone can go to relax in a quiet environment.

5. Review Your Progress

The most important step in doing a digital detox is measuring your progress. You can reflect on your progress each day (preferably at the end of the day) or at the end of each week. Instead of looking for perfection, assess how many small improvements you have made, like not feeling anxious when your phone is in another room or not feeling left behind when you haven't caught up with current affairs. After several detoxes, you can measure the long-term physical and mental benefits reducing technology usage has had on your well-being.

A digital detox isn't about depriving you of technology. It's a way to show you that your life can still function efficiently without it. In other words, your life doesn't depend on technology, although when it is used responsibly, it can make your life feel richer.

LESSON 10: DEFINE SUCCESS ON YOUR OWN TERMS

The difference between a successful person and others is not a lack of strength, not a lack of knowledge, but rather a lack in will.
—Vince Lombardi

WHAT IS SUCCESS?

Success can seem like an abstract concept that one can never seem to get close enough to. When you allow the world around you, including your peers or the media, to influence how you perceive success, you can feel like you are so far away from achieving success in your life. But the truth is success is subjective, meaning it can be anything you desire it to be. Depending on your values, goals, and purpose in life, you can create your own definition of success.

While success is subjective, there are a few myths about achieving success in business that we need to highlight:

1. Following Your Passion Won't Guarantee Success

People are often told that the secret to success is following their passions. This isn't necessarily true. It is possible to fail at something you love or are deeply passionate about. From a business context, it isn't your love for entrepreneurship that guarantees success but your level of skill, innovation, and many other factors. Furthermore, you might be passionate about a product or service, but there isn't a market demand for it; as a result, it doesn't generate a lot of revenue.

2. You Need to Know the Right People to Succeed

I am an advocate for building your professional network, although your success in business doesn't solely rest on having a network. There is a popular saying that "Your network is your net worth," which suggests that who you know has a huge bearing on how far you go in your career. Of course, knowing the right people can open doors for you, but nothing beats building strong relationships with your customers. If you want to impress someone, focus on impressing your customers—not your network. They are the ones with the power to take your business to the next level.

3. You Need an MBA to Get Ahead

Another common myth is that going to business school gives you an advantage as an entrepreneur. This isn't true. I have found that the best teacher is experience and learning from your mistakes. However, this doesn't mean that you shouldn't save up to go to business school if that is one of your education goals. Remember that acquiring knowledge is a lifelong endeavor, so if you aren't attending college, you should certainly be reading different kinds of business books or receiving some type of mentorship.

4. You Need to Invest All of Your Effort Into One Business Venture

Success in business is unpredictable. There are so many factors that need to work in your favor for your business to succeed. Therefore, it isn't a good idea to focus on one business idea or venture. If you can, try to branch out and pursue side business projects while simultaneously growing your main business. You never know which one of your businesses will be your cash cow. Aim to become a serial entrepreneur, like billionaire Sir Richard Branson, who has founded hundreds of companies and struck gold on several of them!

5. Money Is the Marker of Success

A common myth about success is that it can be seen by how much wealth you make in your business or how many materialistic possessions you own. It's true that wealth is one of the signs of success, but it isn't the marker of success. Other factors, like how aligned you are to your purpose or how much impact you make in your community, are also important markers of success. If you look to money alone to define your success, what will happen when your business goes through an unexpected financial crisis? How will you be able to pick yourself up and maintain a positive self-perception when, in your terms, you are suddenly unsuccessful?

So, if success isn't defined by all of these things, how can you define success? I will leave you to decide how you want to define your success, but here are three questions that you can reflect on while you come up with your own definition:

- What are you passionate about?
- What would you desire people to pay you to do it?
- What legacy do you want to leave behind in the world?

Mark Batterson is an author and pastor who has written several books on leadership and success. In an article he wrote titled, "The Definition of Success," he lists several ways to define what success means to you. Here are some of his definitions of success (Batterson, 2009):

- Success is maximizing your God-given abilities.
- Success is doing the best you can, with what you have, wherever you may be.
- Success is being respected by people who know you the best.
- Success is committing yourself to trying until the day you die.

ENJOY THE SMALL WINS

Do you have a strategy in place to keep yourself motivated while working toward achieving your goals? Why not create small milestones that you can honor along the way to success? Your main focus will be to grow your business, but that doesn't mean you need to wait for something huge for you and your team to celebrate your progress!

Besides allowing you to show your team appreciation, celebrating small wins can also be a great way to boost team morale. Your dream team probably works really hard and getting personal recognition for their dedication can be the motivation they need to continue working hard. Celebrating small wins can also emphasize the value in incremental improvement. For example, scoring a big contract is wonderful, but celebrating the journey it took to get there can make the big victory feel more meaningful.

As an entrepreneur, celebrating small wins can help you maintain a positive outlook on your business. It is so easy to get lost in the day-to-day affairs or the challenges you may face that you forget just how far you have come. Every once in a while, you deserve to recognize key milestones in your business and reflect on the positive developments that have been made. Below are a few ways that you can celebrate the small wins in your business:

1. Share Your Plans

Your driven team of employees want to be included as much as possible in your vision for your company. Sharing your strategic plans with them gives them an opportunity to get excited about what the next quarter or year will look like. When sharing your plans, you can also identify key milestones so that your employees know what they are working toward.

2. Celebrate Your Core Values

What makes a company an incredible place to work is its culture. A company culture is based on the core values of a business. To boost team morale and employee performance, you can create milestones that celebrate your core values. For example, if diversity is one of your values, you can set a target to recruit a multicultural team, offer your services in multiple languages, or create your own cultural holidays. These small celebrations can reinforce your commitment to living out your values.

3. Publicly Praise High-Performing Employees

It's important to express how much you value your team. Without them, your business wouldn't run as smoothly as it does. Publicly praising high-performing employees can feel rewarding for the honoree and serve as a source of encouragement for others. Honoring your employees doesn't have to be a costly exercise. You can have an employee of the month initiative where the chosen employee gets an extra hour lunch, free coffee, or a day off.

4. Share Positive Customer Feedback

Research has shown that the most effective praise-to-criticism ratio is 1:6, meaning that for every negative criticism given, you should be giving six positive reviews or compliments. Your positive reviews or compliments don't need to be directed at individuals. For instance, when customers leave positive feedback about the company, you can share them in your workplace meetings; print them and pin them on your bulletin board; or take a screenshot and send it to your work group chat. This will remind your employees that their work is valued by customers.

5. Be There for Each Other

Some small wins are experienced in your employees' personal lives, but that doesn't mean you can't celebrate with them! Create a work environment where your team feels comfortable sharing pet pictures, stories about their kids, birthday announcements, or any major milestones they may be going through in their lives. As a leader, remembering the little things about each employee and being understanding of personal issues can make them feel supported at work.

THINK DIFFERENTLY ABOUT FAILURE

On an episode of *World's Toughest Race: Eco-Challenge Fiji*, a team went down the wrong river on their paddle board and only realized this when they were too far out to turn back. In that moment, you could see in their eyes that they wanted to give up. How could they possibly rectify this situation? However, after the panic had simmered down and the reality of the situation kicked in, they chose to stay in the race, think resourcefully, and carry on!

When you succeed in entrepreneurship one day, no one will remember your low moments. Those who will be celebrating your success with you will tell stories of how much you have inspired them to pursue their dreams and never give up. No one will speak about the rejection, financial struggles, and missed opportunities because your decision to continue pushing forward despite the setbacks is what makes you a living legend!

What makes entrepreneurship intimidating for many aspiring start-up entrepreneurs is the possibility of failure. Let's face it: No one wants to lose at anything, especially when there is hard-earned money invested in it! However, even more than losing, entrepreneurs fear the perceived humiliation that comes with failure. Society has associated failure with weakness and incompetence. However, as leaders, we have gone a step further and defined ourselves by our successes and failures. In other words, we feel confident about ourselves for as long as our businesses are going well, but as soon as challenges arise, we are tempted to quit in order to save face. The truth is that failure is not a sign of weakness or incompetence, and unless we change how we look at it, we will remain gripped by fear.

It's unrealistic to assume that you will never have fears or to believe that you will never face challenges in your business. There will certainly be times when your fears are legitimate, and you are in trouble and don't know what to do. However, how you manage your fears and cope with setbacks has a strong influence on your ability to succeed. Managing fear is all about your mindset and the beliefs you create about your business experiences. At the end of the day, failure is an objective experience. It happened, and you can't take it back, but your mind can create stories about your failure, which turns it into a subjective experience.

There are two common types of mindsets that entrepreneurs have, which can determine their perceptions on failure. The growth mindset causes entrepreneurs to see failure as a type of feedback, and the fixed mindset causes entrepreneurs to see failure as a result of personal inadequacy. When failure is seen as feedback, there is room for development because a new plan or strategy can be implemented. However, when failure is seen as a result of personal limitations, there is no point in trying again because the belief is that you will get the same negative results.

It's not like entrepreneurs with a growth mindset never desire to give up. When things aren't working out and money is tight, that thought certainly enters their minds. However, their openness to learning and adapting their approach to business keeps them in the game. They take a deep breath and realize that one day, they will look back at the hard times and thank themselves for looking fear in the face and just doing it anyway.

Unfortunately, I can't promise that you won't experience hardship on your way to the top. Although, what I can promise you is that if you think differently about the difficulties you encounter, you will develop the mindset and character to ride the storms and come out stronger on the other side. Here are a few tips to help you start changing your outlook on failure:

1. Prepare to Fail

When you anticipate failure, you are less overwhelmed or unprepared if it comes. I'm not saying that you should be pessimistic but rather to be realistic about your plans. There is no plan that is completely risk-free. Even carefully considered plans have some sort of element of risk. By planning ahead of time for the risks you could face, you will have a crisis management plan that you can implement if your Plan A doesn't work. Even if you can't take yourself out of the crisis, at least you would have prepared yourself mentally for the tough times ahead.

2. Reflect on Your Experiences

Get into the habit of reflecting on your experiences—both good and bad. This will increase your level of self-awareness so that you are able to assess situations from multiple perspectives instead of looking at them from your own opinion. Your experiences can also teach you valuable lessons about being a leader and what it takes to run a successful business. You can make reflection a daily practice by writing a page each day in a journal, taking relaxing walks by yourself, or practicing gratitude.

3. Avoid Comparisons

Failure feels much worse when you are subconsciously competing with other businesspeople. Comparing your business journey to someone else's is not only the quickest way to fail but also the quickest way to shatter your self-esteem. Your competitors are not your enemies or people you need to impress. Rather, they are the mentors you never knew you needed! They are there to remind you of the standard of quality, customer service, and innovation that you need to aim for, but that's all. When thinking about your business, see yourself running the race alone.

4. Enjoy the Process

If you base "work" on meeting your goals, you will soon feel discouraged when you experience time delays or realize your goals aren't attainable right now. However, being connected to the small tasks you do on a daily basis can make the journey toward the big goals feel meaningful. Failure won't feel as painful when you are genuinely enjoying the process of running your business. This is because when you enjoy the process, you are less likely to have high expectations for the end result. Look for tasks in your business that you love and don't feel like "work," like meeting clients or creating cool marketing content online. These can be the tasks you work on when you need a boost of confidence and a reminder to never give up.

5. Seek Support

Failure isn't a unique experience. In a room full of entrepreneurs, you would hear plenty of stories of hardships, loneliness, stress, rejection, and battles with mental health. You never have to feel like you have to deal with your challenges alone. There are industry-based professional groups for entrepreneurs online, as well as many public forums, where you can receive advice from people who have been in your position. If the stress of running your business is causing noticeable physical or mental problems, you can speak to a therapist or business coach who can offer you more tailored support.

LIVE FRUGALLY: YOU WON'T REGRET IT

What better way to end off this chapter about success than to tell you how you should spend your money? No, I'm only kidding. You have full control on how you save, spend, or invest the millions you will generate from your start-up. However, I would like to share a lifestyle tip that helped me work my way to a million dollars—one penny at a time.

Frugality tends to get a bad rap in society. Penny-pinchers are usually seen as being stingy with their money, but this isn't true. There is a difference between a stingy and a frugal entrepreneur. A stingy entrepreneur is someone who sees a financial need in their business or personal life but is reluctant to part with their money. A frugal entrepreneur sees a financial need and looks for the most cost-effective ways to respond to it. Frugal entrepreneurs are conscious about their spending habits because they often have huge financial goals. They teach themselves to save rather than spend their money, so they can get closer to achieving their goals.

Frugal entrepreneurs are also not broke. In fact, the opposite is true. Since they have adopted the culture of saving money, they have thousands of dollars either locked away in investments or in their emergency funds. However, over and above saving money, frugality is a lifestyle, and some entrepreneurs go to extreme lengths to save a buck. Here are a few examples of wealthy entrepreneurs who live frugally (Okyle, 2016):

- English businessman, John Caudwell (current net worth of $3.2 billion), reportedly cycled 14 miles to the office and cut his own hair to save money.
- The legendary investor, Warren Buffett (current net worth of $114.3 billion), lives in the same modest home he purchased in 1956.
- Former Microsoft CEO, Steve Ballmer (current net worth of $95.5 billion), has said that he doesn't buy new clothes and prefers to drive a Ford because that's the company his father used to work for.

- The late founder of Ikea, Ingvar Kamprad (net worth of $42.5 billion in 2018), would buy his clothes at local flea markets and often rode on public transport.

So what savings tips can you learn from the world's wealthiest frugal entrepreneurs?

- **Avoid impulsive purchases.** Train yourself to delay swiping your credit card when you want to buy something you don't need. The longer you delay the impulse to purchase something, the less desirable it will become.
- **Live within your means.** When you are living within your means, your expenses don't exceed your income. This means there is little debt you are financing on a month-to-month basis and more money going into your savings.
- **Keep a track record of all your expenses.** Store your receipts and keep track of credit card transactions, so you have an idea of where your money is going. Avoid falling into the trap of thinking you are in the clear just because there is revenue coming in every month. Remember that profit is only calculated after deducting expenses, so keep a watch on your expenses.
- **Create an emergency fund as soon as possible.** Ideally, you should have at least three months' worth of savings set aside for unexpected financial expenses. Each month, you can invest a portion of your profits into your emergency fund so that your business is covered.
- **Avoid risky investments.** Before investing money into a stock or business, assess the level of risk you are exposing yourself to. As a rule of thumb, you should

invest in assets you have knowledge about. Speak to a broker about potential investment opportunities that can help you achieve your financial goals.

CONCLUSION

If someone told me seven years ago that I would have a multimillion e-commerce business today, I wouldn't have believed them. As much as being an entrepreneur and having a successful business was my dream, I didn't believe in myself enough to think it would ever become a reality. After going back and forth with myself about whether or not to take the leap of faith and start my business, I decided to go for it. I didn't want to live with any regrets, so I would either establish my business or die trying!

This was the mindset that kick-started my entrepreneurship journey and continues to motivate me today. I describe it as the start-up mindset, but in actual fact, it can be broken down into 10 different components. We have explored all 10 components in each chapter and the many lessons that each component comes with. To end off, here is a recap of the 10 lessons to overcome your fear and build a successful start-up business:

Lesson 1: Network and Push Doors

Be willing to step out of your comfort zone and make new

connections. Your professional network should consist of people who can add value to your business and give you access to opportunities. If you can't get access to the right people, seeking the best resources online is the next best way to access opportunities.

Lesson 2: Say YES to Taking Risks

Risks are what enable you to grow in the business world. As good as your plans may be, you will never know if they work if you don't have the courage to test them. Remember: When you are passionate about your goals and truly believe in them, the risks you take along the way become worthy sacrifices.

Lesson 3: Don't Just Dream It, Do It

There will never come a point where you feel 100% ready to start your business. Fear and doubt will always be there, telling you that it's safer not to try. However, you have a vision for what you desire in your life, and building a successful business is part of it. Therefore, start before you feel ready and gain experience as you take action.

Lesson 4: Make Learning Your Lifelong Goal

One of the main traits of a growth-oriented entrepreneur is their commitment to continuous learning. Nowadays, there are many different ways to acquire knowledge that are inexpensive and don't involve educational institutions. Find ways to make learning fun by setting learning objectives and goals and applying techniques to absorb, filter, and organize information in your mind.

Lesson 5: Ready, Fire, Aim!

Go easy on yourself when setting expectations for your business and employees. Perfection is an illusion and an unrealistic expectation to have in your company. Instead of seeking perfection, set high expectations that can help you plan effective strategies (getting you Ready), so you can make good decisions (Fire your shot) and work on improving them later (refining your Aim).

Lesson 6: Quitting Is Not an Option

For as long as you keep going, you have the ability to succeed. Entrepreneurship isn't easy, and many times, the factors holding you back are not in your control. But, instead of allowing yourself to get weighed down by things outside of your influence, work on improving the aspects of your business that you can positively change. Your resilience during hard times will build your character and enable you to confidently face whatever comes your way.

Lesson 7: Don't Fear Hard Work

There's a difference between having a good work ethic and working hard. The first is about your attitude toward work, and the other is about the energy you put into your work. Building a start-up business requires you to move! You set the pace and work culture in your company that your employees follow. Nonetheless, overworking yourself sets a bad example and can compromise your mental and physical health. Know when your body needs a break and take as much rest as you need.

Lesson 8: Put Your Strengths to Work

You were born with qualities that make you stand out from a

crowd. Identifying these qualities and using them to your advantage in business can give you a competitive advantage. When recruiting your dream team, look for people who display similar qualities. Ideally, you want a team that can back your vision and use their talents and skills to accelerate your business.

Lesson 9: Avoid Digital Distractions

The amount of convenience technology can offer your business is remarkable but be mindful when using technology in your everyday life. Technology dependency is dangerous and can lead to burnout and depression. Set healthy boundaries for your technology usage, like creating a curfew or going on a digital detox, so you can feel connected to your life.

Lessons 10: Define Success on Your Own Terms

When defining success, consider the things that make you glad to be alive or the goals that are meaningful to you. You don't need to limit success to materialistic possessions or what seems socially acceptable. The small joys of life can bring as much happiness as the large victories that come by once in a while.

With these 10 lessons, you are set to begin the journey of a lifetime—the journey you have waited so long to undertake. You have been given the tools to gradually shift your mindset so you can stay positive and empowered throughout each stage of your business. All that's left to do now is to take action!

REFERENCES

7 Ways how to identify your personal Strengths. (2021, July 29). HIGH5 TEST. https://high5test.com/identifying-personal-strengths/

Abraham Law. (2020, March 16). *What can I do? The circles of concern and influence*. Abraham | Law. https://www.abrahampc.com/blog/2020/3/16/what-can-i-do-the-circles-of-concern-and-influence

Aladesuru, A. W. (2014, June 9). *Sacrifice is the heart of leadership*. Www.linkedin.com. https://www.linkedin.com/pulse/20140609112539-182428527-sacrifice-is-the-heart-of-leadership/

Avery, M. (2016, August 9). *Your definition of success*. Www.linkedin.-com. https://www.linkedin.com/pulse/your-definition-success-matt-avery-mba-ma/

Baron, M. (2014, June 27). *9 "Mindsets" you need to switch from employee to entrepreneur*. Entrepreneur. https://www.entrepreneur.com/article/234894

Batterson, M. (2009, September 21). *The definition of success*. Leaders Leading. https://leadersleading.wordpress.com/2009/09/21/the-definition-of-success/

Buckingham, M. (2010). *Go put your strengths to work : 6 powerful steps to achieve outstanding performance*. Free Press.

Clarke, C. (2016, July 24). *Why curiosity is the most important trait an entrepreneur can have*. Women on Business. https://www.womenonbusiness.com/why-curiosity-is-the-most-important-trait-an-entrepreneur-can-have/

Clear, J. (2012, November 12). *Habits of successful people: Start before you feel ready*. James Clear. https://jamesclear.com/successful-people-start-before-they-feel-ready

Cleveland Clinic. (2021, November 23). *4 Reasons to do a digital detox*. Cleveland Clinic. https://health.clevelandclinic.org/digital-detox/

Cornthwaite, C. (2020, September 18). *11 Boss-level tips on how to network*. Roostervane. https://roostervane.com/tips-on-how-to-network/

Covey, F. (n.d.). *The 7 habits of highly effective people*. Www.franklin-covey.com. https://www.franklincovey.com/the-7-habits/

Dority, K. (2014, January 28). *How can I ask somebody to be my mentor?* Information and Library Jobs. https://www.libgig.com/how-to-ask-someone-to-mentor-you/

Entrepreneur. (2017, August 23). *Never quit: Strategies on perseverance from 5 seasoned entrepreneurs*. Entrepreneur. https://www.entrepreneur.com/article/299071

Farrell, T. (2021, October 14). *Council Post: Why entrepreneurial success requires hard work*. Forbes. https://www.forbes.com/sites/forbesbusinesscouncil/2021/10/14/why-entrepreneurial-success-requires-hard-work/?sh=67a4660d7de0

Ferres, Z. (2015, June 24). *5 Ways to celebrate small wins on your way to world domination*. Entrepreneur. https://www.entrepreneur.com/article/246817

Forleo, M. (2020, February 24). *Should you start before you're ready? 3 Questions to ask yourself*. Marie Forleo. https://www.marieforleo.com/2020/02/start-before-youre-ready/

Good Reads. (n.d.-a). *Barack Obama quote*. Www.goodreads.com. https://www.goodreads.com/author/show/6356.Barack_Obama

Good Reads. (n.d.-b). *Criss Jami quote*. Www.goodreads.com. https://www.goodreads.com/author/show/4860176.Criss_Jami

Good Reads. (n.d.-c). *Lou Holtz quote*. Www.goodreads.com. https://www.goodreads.com/author/show/85179.Lou_Holtz

Good Reads. (n.d.-d). *Michele Jennae quote*. Www.goodreads.com. https://www.goodreads.com/author/show/7123032.Michele_Jennae

Good Reads. (n.d.-e). *Pablo Picasso quote*. Www.goodreads.com. https://www.goodreads.com/author/show/3253.Pablo_Picasso

Good Reads. (n.d.-f). *Quitting quotes (105 quotes)*. Www.goodreads.-com. https://www.goodreads.com/quotes/tag/quitting

Good Reads. (n.d.-g). *Risk Quotes*. Www.goodreads.com. https://www.goodreads.com/quotes/tag/risk

Good Reads. (n.d.-h). *Success quotes (12261 quotes)*. Www.goodread-s.com. https://www.goodreads.com/quotes/tag/success?page=2

Good Reads. (2018). *Brian Tracy quote*. Goodreads.com. https://www.goodreads.com/author/show/22033.Brian_Tracy

Guglielmo, C. (2017, January 9). *10 years ago today: Remembering Steve Jobs make iPhone history*. CNET. https://www.cnet.com/tech/mobile/iphone-at-10-apple-steve-jobs-make-iphone-history-remembering/

Hayes, A. (2021, June 13). *What risks does an entrepreneur face?* Investopedia. https://www.investopedia.com/ask/answers/040615/what-risks-does-entrepreneur-face.asp

HealthXChnage. (2019). *Managing your emotions at work*. Healthx-change.sg. https://www.healthxchange.sg/men/health-work/managing-emotions-work

HoursLogger. (2020, February 17). *Perseverance - The most important quality of entrepreneurs*. Www.hourslogger.com. https://www.hourslogger.com/blog/20/Perseverance+-+The+MOST+Important+Quality+of+Entrepreneurs

How to network like a CEO (a pro). (n.d.). Www.right.com. https://www.right.com/thoughtwire/categories/career-work/how-to-network-like-a-ceo-a-pro

Indeed Editorial Team. (2021, February 23). *Entrepreneurial skills: Definition and examples*. Indeed Career Guide. https://www.indeed.com/career-advice/career-development/entrepreneurial-skills

Laurey, M. (n.d.). *6 Things successful entrepreneurs teach us about frugality*. Https://Www.thedailypositive.com/. https://www.thedailypositive.com/successful-entrepreneurs-lessons-frugality/

Lopes, S. (n.d.). *How to switch from an employee to an entrepreneur mindset*. Www.ellevatenetwork.com. https://www.ellevatenetwork.com/articles/8443-how-to-switch-from-an-employee-to-an-entrepreneur-mindset

Maduro, J. (2021, October 19). *Savvy tips to recruit your startup dream team*. Bplans Blog. https://articles.bplans.com/recruit-startup-team/

Malik, S. (2020, December 7). *Skills transformation for the 2021 workplace*. IBM Training and Skills Blog. https://www.ibm.com/blogs/ibm-training/skills-transformation-2021-workplace/

Mattone, J. (2019, March 4). *High expectations vs. Unrealistic expectations: Leadership's fine line*. John Mattone Global, Inc. https://johnmattone.com/blog/high-expectations-vs-unrealistic-expectations-leaderships-fine-line/

MentorCruise. (2021, September 28). *50 Questions to ask a mentor for a great mentorship experience*. Mentorcruise.com. https://mentorcruise.com/blog/22-questions-ask-mentor-great-mentorship-experienc/

Moore, E. (2021, December). *How to ask someone to be your mentor*. Www.glassdoor.com. https://www.glassdoor.com/blog/how-to-ask-someone-to-be-your-mentor/

Mungoshi, J. (2020, August 24). *Ready Fire Aim: Essential elements to getting results*. Www.linkedin.com. https://www.linkedin.com/pulse/ready-fire-aim-essential-elements-getting-results-jonah-mungoshi/

Myatt, M. (2010, September 7). *Leadership and perfectionism*. N2Growth. https://www.n2growth.com/en_za/the-need-for-speed/

Narendra. (2019, August 24). *5 Noteworthy signs you are addicted to technology*. Health Works Collective. https://www.healthworkscollective.com/5-noteworthy-signs-you-are-addicted-to-technology/

OkCredit. (2020, November 20). *How to identify a business opportunity in your locality? Read here*. OkCredit Blogs. https://okcredit.in/blog/how-to-identify-a-business-opportunity/

Okyle, C. (2016, April 18). *Lifestyles of the rich and frugal: 7 Thrifty millionaires and billionaires*. Entrepreneur. https://www.entrepreneur.com/slideshow/272376

Olive. (2014, September 30). *Putting your strengths to work*. Random Olive. https://www.randomolive.com/2014/09/putting-your-strengths-to-work/

Patel, D. (2017, June 15). *7 Big myths about success you need to ignore*. Entrepreneur. https://www.entrepreneur.com/article/293546

Patel, S. (2013, April 16). *The truth about hard work and entrepreneurial success.* Sujan Patel. https://sujanpatel.com/business/the-truth-about-hard-work-and-entrepreneurial-success/

Paul, R. (2020, April 23). *8 Ways to fight entrepreneurial procrastination.* StartUp Mindset. https://startupmindset.com/fight-entrepreneurial-procrastination/#:~:text=A%20fear%20of%20failure%20can

Peter, T. J., & Waterman, R. H. (2004). *In search of excellence : Lessons from America's best-run companies.* Harpercollins Publishers.

Pickard-Whitehead, G. (2020, April 10). *Famous hard work quotes for motivation - 60 of them!* Small Business Trends. https://smallbiztrends.com/2019/08/famous-hard-work-quotes.html

Pierre-Bravo, D. (2018, May 30). *John Paul DeJoria's journey from homeless to billionaire.* MSNBC.com. https://www.msnbc.com/know-your-value/john-paul-dejoria-s-journey-homeless-billionaire-n825246

Raman, N. (2016, April 15). *5 Painful risks if you stop learning something new each day.* Neelraman.com. https://neelraman.com/5-painful-risks-if-you-stop-learning-something-new-each-day/

Robinson, R. (2020, September 29). *8 Steps to discover your strengths as an entrepreneur.* RyRob.com. https://www.ryrob.com/discover-strengths-entrepreneur/

Scroggs, L. (n.d.). *Getting things done: Your step-by-step guide.* Todoist. https://todoist.com/productivity-methods/getting-things-done

Shore, J. (2014, June 19). *Transform your vision into action with these 3 steps*. Entrepreneur. https://www.entrepreneur.com/article/234928

Startup Sloth. (2021, March 14). *Celebrating small wins: The benefits of celebrating success, no matter how small*. Startup Sloth. https://startupsloth.com/celebrating-small-wins-the-benefits-of-celebrating-success-no-matter-how-small/

Statista. (2022, January 11). *E-learning: global market size by segment*. Statista. https://www.statista.com/statistics/1130331/e-learning-market-size-segment-world-wide/#:~:text=In%202019%2C%20the%20global%20online

Swenson, B. (2020, December 3). *Technology: The good, the bad, the ugly*. University of Arkansas Grantham. https://www.uagrantham.edu/blog/technology-the-good-the-bad-the-ugly/

Sykes, T. (2019, November 8). *The 1 thing you must control to be successful*. Entrepreneur. https://www.entrepreneur.com/article/341901

Tarver, E. (2021, August 30). *Mark Zuckerberg success story: Net worth, education and influence*. Investopedia. https://www.investopedia.com/articles/personal-finance/081315/mark-zuckerberg-success-story-net-worth-education-top-quotes.asp

Taube, A. (2014, December 5). *17 People whose incredible work ethic paid off*. Business Insider. https://www.businessinsider.com/17-hard-working-successful-people-2014-12?IR=T

The Young Entrepreneur Council. (2022, January 31). *15 Signs you're working too much and burning out*. Lifehack. https://www.lifehack.org/articles/lifehack/ask-the-entrepreneurs-15-signs-youre-working-too-much-and-burning-out.html

U.S. Bureau of Labor Statistics. (2022, February 1). *Job openings and labor turnover summary*. Bls.gov. https://www.bls.gov/news.release/jolts.nr0.htm

Valamis. (2019, March 27). *Continuous learning*. Valamis.com. https://www.valamis.com/hub/continuous-learning

Walsh, S. (2018, April 7). *10 Tips for better continuous learning*. Anders Pink. https://blog.anderspink.com/2018/04/10-tips-continous-learning/

Wang, D. (2020, July 1). *"I was rejected from Harvard 10 times", Alibaba founder Jack Ma on persistence*. Boss Hunting. https://www.bosshunting.com.au/hustle/rejected-from-harvard-10-times-alibaba-jack-ma/#:~:text=He%20failed%20his%20university%20entrance

ABOUT THE AUTHOR

Pete Moon

Pete Moon is a Reluctant Entrepreneur, Aspiring Publisher and Founder of 'Moonster Handmade Leather' - 7 Figure Global E-Commerce Business. He started out with a next-to-useless Media Degree at Cardiff University in the UK. He went back to study again at a Bible College, then swiftly 'failed' at becoming a Pastor. This led him to retrain as a plumber/kitchen fitter and then set up his first company. In his "spare time" (burning the candle at both ends), he began to build a second business from scratch - what is now a multi million physical products business, selling in 10 online marketplaces worldwide. Currently Pete is working on a third digital products ecom business and is always dreaming about other possible future startups.

Printed in Great Britain
by Amazon

25024668R00081